THRIVING THROUGH SEASONS OF GRIEF

How to Overcome in
Life's Disappointments,
Change and Loss

KATHLEEN MAXWELL-RAMBIE

Christian Faith
PUBLISHING

ISBN 978-1-0980-4210-3 (paperback)
ISBN 978-1-0980-4212-7 (digital)

Christian Faith Publishing, Inc.
832 Park Avenue
Meadville, PA 16335
www.christianfaithpublishing.com

Printed in the United States of America

For Stephen, my husband, for your love,
support, and fun adventures.

For my children, Austin, Mallory and Price, I'm so proud of
how you have navigated and walked life without your Dad.

And in memory of Joe Maxwell and Landon and Mary Belle Jones.

Contents

Endorsements for Thriving Through Seasons of Grief

Cassie Alex

If you are walking through any kind of pain from loss or find yourself helping someone navigate through the rough waters of grief, Kathleen's book, "Thriving Through Seasons of Grief," is for you!!! As a Hospice Director for many years, I have read almost every book out there on grief. This is one of the best. Kathleen's fresh approach doesn't just take you on her journey through her losses; she gives you the stepping stones, tools, and promises you will need to make it through your own personal journey. She calls it the "Price of Love". The process of grief doesn't come with a map, calendar, or a flashlight but the words in this book will guide you to identify the types of grief you are feeling and help you understand the Challenges, the Benefits, the Healing, the Hope, the Promises, and How to Thrive Again! Having sat in the bleachers watching Kathleen walk through some of the deepest pain of loss, to listening to her teachings, and reading her writings, this book is a testament to the depth, strength, and integrity of an amazing God Loving Woman. We will definitely stock our shelves with this valuable book to use as tools to help our patient's families and our friends.

Cassie Alex
New Century Hospice Kerrville
Director of Operations

Lisa Davis

This is an engaging read. I highly recommend this book to any reader experiencing grief. Seldom do you find a book that is both highly instructive, and truly inspiring at the same time. Kathleen provides practical advice and inspiring stories how God helped her triumph over adversity. "Sometimes the only way to heal is to fall apart, and let God remake you." I highly recommend this book to read and share with others.

Lisa Davis, RN
Hospice Nurse for 10 years

Teri Schreiner

Kathleen Maxwell-Rambie became my friend and Christian mentor over 30 years ago. Over that period of time we have shared some of life's biggest blessings, and we have also shared some of life's most unfortunate tragedies. In 2014, I found myself widowed, in 2017, I suffered another great loss, and in 2019 my home of 20 years burned to the ground. Because Kathleen has walked through her own losses and grief, she was able to share with me the faith and wisdom that she learned along the way which in turn, has given me understanding, courage, and hope for my own journey.

I have found Kathleen's new book, Thriving Through Seasons of Grief, to be extremely comprehensive. In it, she covers the stages and types of grief, what to expect and how to care for yourself and others. She talks about forgiveness and why that is so important in the healing process and even provides scriptures to help us focus on God's truth instead of lies or our own emotions. It is very honest and relatable and is based on Kathleen's own experiences, as well as those of others.

This is the first book on grief that I have read (and I have read a lot!) that focuses on not just surviving, but THRIVING in grief. Although grief is never a positive experience or something anyone wants to go through, this book challenges us to look for the positive and to try and grow in it, both personally and spiritually.

Teri Schreiner
The Gathering Leadership Team
Business Owner, and widow

Franklin Williamson

As a pastor who has counseled people with various stages of grief, this book is a must read. And especially for anyone who is held in its agonizing grip. Also, it is for everyone, as it will help prepare us all, for what is yet to come, as we experience loss of loved ones and the ups and downs in life.

The book is very inciteful and well written from a person who has experienced various forms of grief. The book gives a thorough understanding of what grief is, the different kinds of grief, the stages of grief and gives a pathway out. It is very encouraging and gives hope as it explains the positive and uplifting benefits of grief. I highly recommend "Thriving Through Seasons of Grief" even for those who have not yet experienced all of its ramifications.

Franklin Williamson
Pastor and Director of Treasure Commission

Katie Bess Williamson

Kathleen Maxwell-Rambie has written a book that many can identify with and will be comforted by her experiences and her understanding of the process of grief.

Everyone will experience the loss of a person they love at some time in their life and her book is a guide for what to expect in the grieving process.

It also will be helpful for understanding the emotions that a person will experience, in a time of grief. She has written a book that will be beneficial to everyone at any stage of their lives. The book also enables us to understand what others might be experiencing in their loss of any kind. I highly recommend this book for everyone.

Katie Bess Williamson
Pastoral Care, Counselor, and Business Owner

Allison Bown

I have known Kathleen Maxwell-Rambie personally and in ministry for many years. She has not only walked this journey herself but allowed Jesus to walk it with her and has been transformed by the experience. Because of that, her writing is like having a compassionate and strong friend come up and take your arm, saying, "I'll walk through this with you." The truths here are a beautiful balm to a battered heart. Her chapters are concise because she remembers that in a time of grief, you can't process a great deal.

Her writing gives permission to go at your own pace, understanding that everyone's journey will be unique. It gently disassembles the walls of isolation that "I must be the only one" or "If I was stronger, I would be over this."

Kathleen makes no demands. She only gives gifts… beautiful, compassionate, strengthening gifts of grace and hope that bring life and freedom.

Allison Bown
Creative Partner at Brilliant Perspectives
and author of "Joyful Intentionality" and "The Image"
Brilliantbookhouse.com

Frankie and Denise Enloe

Kathleen shares her grief journey with honesty and hope through unique spiritual insight. God answered her prayer by allowing the pain of loss to not be in vain by giving her this opportunity to encourage and support others on their journey.

Frankie Enloe, Pastor Turtle Creek Community
Church and wife, Denise Enloe

Introduction

It was a hot summer day in 2009 and Joe, my late husband, and I were sitting in our living room. He was battling a rare cancer, Merkel Cell Carcinoma, and was recovering from a surgery that removed a nineteen-centimeter tumor from his shoulder. He had lost function of his right arm.

Shortly after his diagnosis, Joe began a Caring Bridge site, to keep our family, friends, coworkers, and community people informed on how to pray and where we were in our battle. Both of us had grown up here in Kerrville, Texas and been active in the Hill Country.

"Joe, people are asking for an update. If you will tell me what to say, I will write it for you," I stated, as I sat down at the computer.

"No, I want you to share what is on your heart. God has something for you in writing," he replied in a soft but firm voice.

"Well, I will write until you get better, but I didn't even like English or writing in high school or college," I replied back. "I am not a writer." I continued.

In the days and weeks ahead, Joe did not get better, and the news we received was not good. We had so many people around the world cheering us on in our battle for his life, praying and believing with us for healing. God had done many great things for us since he was diagnosed that cold day, January 8, 2009.

I did not want to share all the negative news without also showing how faithful God had been to us during our battle. The ten-hour surgery at MD Anderson was not the cure we had hoped for and the cancer had spread.

> The negative news was only part of our story. Watching someone I love suffer is the hardest thing I have endured, and yet, I was learning the beauty of walking with God through the "valley of the shadow of death."

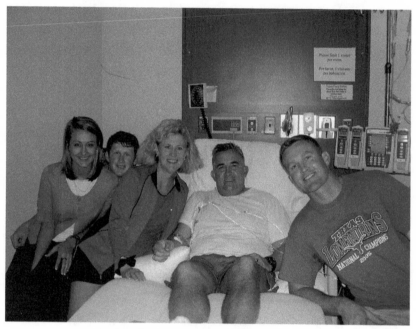

Our family battling cancer in 2009

Last Maxwell family vacation in 2009

Joe Maxwell

Joe's health continued to decline, so I began to share my heart in a transparent way and also shared the goodness of God, when our prayers did not get answered the way we wanted. As I continued to tell our story on the Caring Bridge site, hundreds of people began following our site and little did I know, I was beginning my calling as a writer.

Early on the morning of October 8, 2009, nine months to the day after diagnosis, Joe took his last breath on earth and his first breath in heaven.

After his death, I continued sharing my heart and my journey through grief on Caring Bridge. We had over 39,950 visits to this website.

Toward the end of 2009, my children suggested I transition to a blog, www.themaxwellminutes.blogspot.com, as many were responding and people were identifying with overcoming difficulty. People were looking for encouragement during hard times, and all of us encounter adversity. I continued writing about grief, life without Joe, and how God was faithful in my journey through grief.

One day, in January of 2010, a young editor of the faith section of *The Kerrville Daily Times*, contacted me. Her name was Carlina Villapando, and she had been following our Caring Bridge website and my blog. Carlina encouraged me in my writing and asked me to begin writing for the faith section of the paper. She later became the editor and publisher of *The Kerrville Daily Times*.

"I'm not a writer," I told her, but I did agree to pray about it and loved the opportunity to share about who God was. In March of 2010, I began writing for the paper and shortly after that, *The Hill Country Community Journal.* Ten years later, I write for three newspapers, my blog, lead a community Bible study called The Gathering-Bringing God into Everyday Life, and have a podcast, kathleenmaxwellrambie.podbean.com.

I discovered the veil between life and death is very thin. Joe saw me in the future. He saw me through God's eyes, and I believe Carlina heard from God and saw my potential. I do not think I would have ever begun writing or speaking if Joe and I had not had that conversation in our living room in July of 2009 and without Carlina's invitation. I am grateful for both of them.

This book is dedicated to my late husband, Joe Maxwell, for his kindness, love, encouragement, and always believing in me. He was such a great cheerleader in my life. It is also dedicated to the friends that have heard God and encouraged me to overcome the adversity and rise above it. I am forever grateful.

I also want to dedicate it to the man I married in 2012, Stephen Rambie. He has given me the opportunity to live a whole new life, a lot of fun, and great adventures.

> **God has opened many doors to speak, write, and share about many things with many people and to encourage them in their walk through tough times. Grief is a part of life on this earth. All of us will find ourselves in seasons of grief and I pray you will not waste the heartache. Let God shape you, grow through the difficulty, and discover the new life God has for you.**

October 8, 2019, marked the ten-year anniversary of Joe's death. It seems like yesterday, and yet it seems like a lifetime ago. I am a different woman than I was ten years ago, and the grief process has changed me in many positive ways.

A new compassion and talent developed in my time and during my journey through grief. I am passionate about helping people, and I pray you will find beauty in the ashes of whatever adversity you are going through right now and healing of your heart, for the grief you have been through in your life.

In the meantime, trust God and hang on to Romans 8:28 (KJV), "And we know all things work together for good to them that love God, to them who are the called according to his purpose."

Kathleen Maxwell-Rambie

Chapter 1

Don't Waste the Pain

"God, if I have to go through this pain, I don't want to waste it," I muttered under my breath as I walked through my neighborhood trying to figure out what happened to my life.

I had married my high school sweetheart when I was nineteen, so married life was all that I knew as an adult. Joe and I had been married thirty years and were looking forward to being empty nesters when he died at age fifty-two.

I knew a little about grief from a miscarriage I had years ago and other losses in my life, but what I was experiencing now that he was gone was so hard. When I thought about the future without him, it literally made it hard to breathe at times.

Previous grief experiences had been great teachers in my life, and I knew there was gold to be found in this heartbreak and the road ahead, however, I really was not excited about the journey.

"God, let grief have a good work in my life and keep me moving in the process," I prayed. *"Work things out of me that need to go and work things into me that will make me more like you."*

I did not want to just go through the pain and not come out different. I also did not want to get stuck in the grief process.

Things happen in life that can cause our hearts to hurt or break, and no one is exempt; however, what we do during these times in our lives is crucial to our well-being.

Psalms 23:3 (NIV) says, "Even though I walk *through* the darkest valley, I will fear no evil, for you are with me; your rod and your staff, they comfort me."

I will share about God, not to preach to anyone, but He was a big part of my grief journey. When we leave this earth and know Jesus, we go to a place of love. In my losses, cognitively, I understood my loved ones were in a better place; however, I was left to pick up the pieces of life. *Thankfully, God was closer than I realized, and I was not alone in my journey.*

It was comforting to me to realize that God's heart was not for me to stay in a state of heartache and grief and it was His desire for me to go *through* this valley, and He was with me. Again, I was not alone.

There were times in the days ahead that I had to literally picture myself holding Jesus' hand as I walked during the day and dealt with many things that were previously my husband's responsibility.

God was faithful to take me up on those prayers and in the pages that follow, I will share the many treasures I found in my grief journey. I will also share how God changed me, shaped me, and taught me how to *thrive* in grief, and hopefully, it will encourage and help you in your journey.

There are many neat things I have discovered in processing my heartbreak and grief.

1. I feel I know the heart of God in a way I never knew Him before.
2. Sometimes the only way to heal, is to fall apart, and let God remake you.
3. Releasing built up emotions allows a cleansing opportunity that prepares the way for positive deposits in our lives, so as you read, let the tears roll, I give you permission to cry.
4. Grief has been one of the best teachers in my life.
5. What you do in your own grief journey will make a big difference positively or negatively in your life and the lives of others.

As you read and process, my prayer is that you will walk away with tools in your tool belt of life and learn what grief is, how it affects us, challenges of grief, benefits of grief and how to partner with the process. I also pray that any lies you have previously believed about the process will unravel, and you will receive another layer of healing for your heart. Most of all, I pray that you will discover how to *thrive in seasons of grief.*

Chapter 2

Who Signs Up for Grief?

In 2017, I was asked to speak about grief for the Dynamic Learning Institute, a community lifelong learning program in Kerrville, Texas. I had been writing for the local newspaper and had shared many things about grief, overcoming heartache, and adversity in our newspaper. When I was asked to speak on grief, my first response was "I'm afraid no one will come, people don't sign up for grief."

The truth is, no one signs up for grief, it knocks on the door of our life and intrudes in our life. It is usually unannounced and unwanted. But it is there. So what do we do when this uninvited guest shows up?

Grief is a part of life here on earth and has been around for thousands of years. Why don't people talk about it, I often wondered.

One of the misconceptions people have when going through seasons of grief is that something unusual is happening to them.

Actually, death, loss, and grief is a part of life. What are we going to do when it arrives on our doorstep? How we approach and respond to it makes a big difference in our lives. It can either make us bitter or better.

Learning to partner with God in the process became my biggest asset in life.

> **When we embrace grief, it can be one of our best teachers and can shape us in many positive ways.**

I grew up in a home where I was taught to "suck it up, be tough, you're a Jones." It was not okay to show emotion or tears, as they were a sign of weakness.

I lived much of my life that way until a series of events, disappointment and loss happened in my thirties and then I just could not "suck it up" anymore.

As I talked with a dear friend about what I was feeling, she reassured me and said, "Kathleen, you are perfectly normal. You are just going through grief."

Those days began my discovery about the process and benefits of grief. I also quickly discovered that many people do not talk about grief or their feelings. They pretend they do not hurt, and a large number of people do not know how to help and understand grieving people.

Chapter 3

What Is Grief?

Grief is the process of letting go, saying goodbye to a person or season in our lives and moving on to what God has for us.

Letting go of the grief, sorrow, or disappointment is vital to moving forward in our lives. The letting go is not always easy, as in many instances, it is saying goodbye to a part of our lives that will never be again. Facing and embracing that reality is oftentimes hard and takes courage.

If we do not deal with our grief, it can oftentimes lead to unhealthy behaviors such as emotional outburst, anger, anxiety, addictions, or depression.

No one is exempt from the process. It does not matter who you are, how much money you have, or how much you know; each person is responsible for how they go through the process of grief. And let me emphasize the word *process*. Grief is often not a quick event in our lives but a process.

Understanding grief and the process is a huge key in learning to embrace the process and thriving through the process. In my own journey, it was comforting to know that what I was experiencing was simply part of the healing process.

Grief has a way of bringing us to a place where we are confronted with the fact that we do not have all the answers anymore and this is good. There are just some things in life we cannot figure out or understand, and it is okay.

Below are some feelings and behaviors of a grieving person. Perhaps you will recognize some of them:

- sadness
- sorrow
- anger
- guilt
- confusion
- forgetfulness
- things we can normally handle, we cannot
- thirst
- not sleeping well
- little or no appetite

If you discover you can identify with any of the above things, let them be something positive. These symptoms can be like a flag waving to notify you; you need to process your grief.

Anticipatory Grief

Anticipatory grief occurs when one realizes someone is dying, slipping away, or the end of a season is approaching, unless a miracle occurs.

My mother, Mary Belle, was a 5'2" vivacious and beautiful woman. When she contracted a rare autoimmune disease, it affected not only her physically but also cognitively. Watching her slowly decline was very painful, and I shed many tears.

One day, I was sharing my heart with a friend, that was also a counselor, and stated that I just did not think my heart could handle the strain, as I knew my mom would die soon. I was relieved when she told me that I was dealing with anticipatory grief, and actually, I was grieving in installments. This was encouraging to me as I was dreading more intense emotional pain when she died.

My mom was sick for nine years, and I let go of her a little each year. I grieved when it became apparent that I was the parent, and now, she was the child. I grieved that she could not function like a normal adult and was not "there for me anymore."

When she passed away, it hurt, but most of my grief was dealt with as I had nine years of letting go.

Let me stress that you can grieve your situation and still be believing in faith for the healing of your loved one. In my journey through grief, I learned that letting go did not mean I had given up hope.

> **To me, it meant I was embracing where I was, trusting God, and letting go to move forward in my life, even though the future was unknown.**

Anticipatory grief is not running from the unfortunate possibilities but accepting where you are in order to move forward.

Compounded Grief

Sometimes life hits hard, and there can be multiple things to grieve. My mother had been sick for years, and I was slowly watching her life slip away. The grief over her condition would come and go. Then my husband died, and six weeks after that, my dad was in Texsan Heart Hospital with a 90 percent blockage in his heart. I began to face the fact that another major man in my life could be gone soon, and there was much to get in order for my parents.

I decided to resign from a job that I dearly loved in order to help my parents and to rest. Grief had taken its toll on my life. Again, another letting go.

Also, there was another organization that was very important to me and my late husband. The simple fact that he was gone and misunderstandings that surround grief (you do not really understand what you have never experienced) changed my status in the organization. It was another letting go and grief in my life.

All these life events compounded the grief. There were multiple things to process, figure out, let go of, forgive, and heal. It made the grief process slower than I liked and difficult; however, I was so thankful someone pointed this out to me. I was dealing with compounded grief. That simple fact brought great understanding and comfort to my heart. I was not just dealing with the loss of my husband but multiple losses. I learned in this season, I had to be kind to me, take special care of myself, be diligent to let go and not only focus on what I had lost, and seek God for healing. I had encountered many losses in a short amount of time.

Perhaps you have now discovered that you too are dealing with multiple losses. Let me encourage you to take one day at a time and be patient with yourself. You will not overcome unless you process each grief, and that takes time. *Everyone wants the pain to be over. However, it is in the process; we heal and grow.*

For about nine months to a year, I took an antidepressant to help me through this difficult time. I am not a person that thinks drugs are the answer and was reluctant at first, but understood. I was dealing with a lot of loss at one time and was grateful for those that helped me process my grief.

The challenge during this time was life went on for people around me. There were those in my life, community, and church that I thought understood grief, and yet they had not experienced it. How could they understand something they had not experienced?

Grief is also a time we have to extend grace to others, especially because we need grace ourselves. I encourage you to ask God to help you extend grace to those around you and give away what you need most in your own life. Challenging, *yes*, but you can do it!

Stuck in Grief Versus Moving Forward in the Process

Too many times, people focus on their loss with a victim mentality. Why did this happen to me?

> **I have found the why question keeps you stuck in moving through the process.**

In 2003, I stepped into full time ministry as director of the Christian Women's Job Corps of Kerr County, an organization that works with women to teach them job and life skills. My mother had prayed for me for years and saw a call on my life, and I was finally doing the things God had destined me to do.

A few short months after I took the job, my mom became very ill. She began to deteriorate physically as well as cognitively, and we discovered she had a rare autoimmune disease.

I questioned God and kept asking why. Why her? Why now? Why haven't you healed her?

I wrestled for months with these questions, until one day, a friend said to me, *"Kathleen, the question is, can you still trust God and live the question, even if you never get an answer."*

I had to ponder that for a while before I could say, "Yes, God, I will trust you even if I never get an answer to these questions."

I then began to focus on "what." What did God want to work in me and out of me? This became my focus as I walked in this process of letting go of the mother that I knew.

Scripture tells us in Romans 8:28 (NIV), "And we know that in *all things* God *works for* the *good* of those who love him, who have been called according to his purpose."

As hard as it was watching my mom change and slip away, God was so faithful to me and taught me much about not having to have answers to things I did not understand. I am forever grateful for the new level of learning to trust Him I gleaned. I learned to lean on God and His ability instead of depending and leaning on my mother.

> **Ask God the question, "What do you want to work in me and out of me," instead of "Why did this happen to me?" The why question can keep you stuck.**

Chapter 4

Different Types of Grief

Death

There are many different kinds of grief a person can experience in life. The obvious kind of grief is the death of a loved one, a child, a spouse, a dear friend, significant other, parent or grandparent. The death can be either expected or unexpected. Death is hard because it is final. Life as we knew it is over, and it is permanent on earth.

Sometimes the process of leaving this earth takes a while and watching my mother slowly decline and watching my late husband suffer during their illnesses has been one of the hardest things I have endured in my lifetime.

When a person has a relationship with Jesus, I believe there is life after death. Scripture tells us we will be reunited with our loved ones when Christ returns.

> After that, we who are still alive and are left will be caught up together with them in the clouds to meet the Lord in the air. And so, we will be with the Lord forever. Therefore encourage one another with these words. (1 Thessalonians 4:17–18, NIV)

Major Change in Season of Life

This type of grief can occur when there is a major shift in our lives, such as the sale of a business we had a long time and invested a great deal of our time and energy into it. I have also seen many people encounter grief when they retire. They usually go from eight-to-twelve-hour days of intense work to a very laid back and different schedule and circle of people.

Losing a job with a company you have worked for a long time can also trigger a season of grief.

When I sold my business of fourteen years, Gymnastics Etc., I encountered feelings and emotions of grief. My late husband and I sold this business, so I could dedicate more time to our children, but I will never forget the day we walked out of the courthouse, after we transferred the name of the business to the new owners.

I turned and looked at Joe and said, "Who am I now? Everyone knows me as Kathleen Maxwell, Gymnastics, Etc., and I just sold my name."

I had invested so much of my energy, time, and heart into building a great business, and now, I was in a place of letting it go. Even though we had chosen to sell, it was a change of season, and I had to let go so I could move into the next season of my life.

At first, I felt lost, unsettled and not sure about being a full time stay at home mom. In this grief, like others, I had to say goodbye, embrace the fact that my life would be different, and discover a new rhythm.

I also experienced grief when I resigned from my job as executive director of the Christian Women's Job Corps of Kerr County. I loved my job and the many volunteers and women that were my clients. I had invested countless hours building this ministry and was passionate about my job; however, I knew I had accomplished what I was called to do.

Both my parents were ill, and there was much that needed to be done in overseeing their care and getting their affairs in order. My late husband had only been gone a year at this time, so my life had already changed dramatically in the recent months.

Letting go of my hectic schedule and something I was passionate about was a huge shift for my daily routine. I needed to rest, process my own grief, and help my parents, but I missed life as I knew it and the daily interaction with the volunteers and clients.

Although I knew in my heart, I had completed what I was called to do for this organization, the letting go was difficult. I knew my parents only had months left to live, and I needed to invest in this precious time with them, nevertheless, there was a grief process in letting go of doing something I dearly loved.

Moving to a New Location

I grew up in Kerrville, Texas, and lived there most of my life. We had friends, work colleagues, church relationships, and people that we socialized with in our community. We had our rhythm in Kerrville and knew who we could trust and call on in time of need. My late husband was offered a job in another community about 120 miles away. It seemed like a good deal for his career and our family, so he accepted the position.

It was hard letting go of all that was comfortable for us, and I noticed a sadness in all of our family, as we said goodbye to friends and the only home my children had known.

Our new community welcomed us; however, there was a season where we had to grieve what was comfortable and the things we missed about Kerrville.

I remember sitting in the Walmart parking lot in our new community, crying. In Kerrville, our community was relatively small, and I would always meet several people I knew and visit with them while shopping. As I shopped in my new location, I did not know a soul. I missed all my friends, acquaintances, and what was familiar. As I sat in the parking lot with tears streaming down my face, I gave the sorrow to God in a simple prayer.

"God, I miss my friends, my community, running into people I know and visiting," I prayed. "I give you my sorrow and ask you to help me embrace my new community and find friends."

I also noticed grief in my children. One day, not long after we moved, my son came home from school and threw himself on his bed and expressed his sorrow. He missed his buddies, his basketball team, and his school. I could not fix it; however, I could offer comfort and encouragement.

> **Letting go and letting the tears roll in grief is important.**

It is releasing our sorrow, and that is healthy. It is also important to hang on to hope and keep taking steps to build our future.

It is okay to miss what we have lost, but it is not healthy to stay in that place and keep looking backwards all the time. We must look forward with expectancy to the next adventure.

Isaiah 43:18–19 (NIV) tells us, "Forget the former things; do not dwell on the past. See, I am doing a new thing! Now it springs up; do you not perceive it? I am making a way in the wilderness and streams in the wasteland."

Of course, we are going to miss what is comfortable and what we have lost in the transition of moving; however, keeping our focus on what is ahead will create an anticipation and expectancy in our hearts.

Death of a Dream

My late husband Joe and I married young. I was nineteen and he was twenty-two. Like many couples, we had our five-year plan for our new life together and eighteen months after we were married, we were expecting our first child. We were excited and surprised that our family was beginning sooner than we expected.

We often talked about how we would still be young and have a little more money once our three kids were grown and our nest was empty. We dreamed about our travels, the fun we would have, and our second honeymoon.

Our last child, Price, left for college in the fall of 2008. We were so excited to begin the season we had dreamed of for years, when all of a sudden in January of 2009, we discovered Joe had a rare cancer, Merkel Cell Carcinoma.

We were quickly thrust into a world of cancer, chemo treatments, doctors' appointments and traveling to MD Anderson in Houston, Texas.

Although traveling to MD Anderson was not our plan, we made the most of it, and those were precious times. We made the most of the last nine months of our lives together. We often talked, laughed, and cried together as we began the grief process of letting go of our dream of what this season of our lives would look like.

After he was gone, one of the things that was difficult for me to grieve and embrace was that we would never have the season of laughter, fun, and travel we had dreamed of.

In my process of letting go, there were many days I would mutter a prayer, "God, I let go of our dream and choose to trust you." Sometimes seeing other couples about our age and older, laughing and having fun was painful, but I continued to release my pain and trust God. I knew I had to let go and grieve the death of our dream in order to move forward in my life.

A few years after Joe's death, I met a wonderful guy, Stephen Rambie and remarried in 2012. He is a very fun-loving, adventurous guy and my daughter, Mallory, said to me one day, "Mom, I know this season of your life did not turn out like you thought for you and Dad, but I think it is neat that you and Stephen travel so many fun places, and you are still getting to realize your dream even though it is not with Dad."

Stephen and Kathleen's wedding

God was faithful to me, and I am forever grateful for the fun season of many travels, fishing and hunting trips, and adventures Stephen and I share. I have learned many new things in my new life, and these years have been even more than I anticipated and dreamed about. My dream just looks different.

Kathleen and Stephen bass fishing in Mexico

Another loss of a dream is infidelity. When your mate is unfaithful, it is a death of the marriage you thought you had. I had a woman share her feelings with me about when she learned of the infidelity; she could not even cry. The shock kept her heart protected until she could process what had just happened in her life. At first, she had difficulty believing the breach of trust and commitment had occurred; however, weeks later, all the stages of grief began as she processed what her husband had done. She was experiencing the death of what she thought her marriage was and would be.

God healed their marriage, but grieving her losses, were very important, so the healing could begin in her life.

Losing a Pet

I am not a huge animal lover or pet person; however, my late husband bought an adorable black and white American Cocker Spaniel that we named Maggie. She was primarily his dog until he passed away.

Not long after Joe was gone, I looked at Maggie and said, "Something else has got to breathe in this house and you are it, Maggie."

This dog quickly became an inside dog and my constant companion for years. She became part of the family in a new way, and my friend, especially during the dark days of losing my husband. When I would cry, she would always get up from wherever she was and move close to me to comfort me.

Maggie lived for seventeen years. The last several years of her life, she began to decline. I found myself distancing myself from her, emotionally and physically, knowing she would not be around long.

The day she died was gut-wrenching as I said goodbye and walked out of the vet's office after putting her down. I had been saying goodbye for a while, but for me, this was the final goodbye of my four-footed companion.

Grief Due to Physical Challenges and Changes

I watched my mom grieve when she got sick, and her body began to drastically change due to her illness. She had to let go of her high heels, something she wore many days in her life and wear, as she called them, "ugly shoes." She was unable to do many things she once enjoyed and had to let go of life as she knew it. It was not easy for her; however, she did it with grace and beauty.

When my grandson, Truett, was two years old, he was diagnosed with type 1 diabetes. It was huge shock to our family, and suddenly, my daughter and son-in-law were thrust into a new world they had not planned on—a medical world that was necessary to keep their son alive with insulin, needles, and the constant monitoring of his blood sugar. There were so many life changes that occurred that cold day in December, that he was diagnosed.

Every parent wants the best for their children, and this was not their plan, nor was it mine as his grandmother. Shortly after his diagnosis, my daughter, Mallory, and I had conversations about grieving, reframing the plans they had for Truett, and what they expected their lives to look like with this news. My daughter had a million questions going through her mind as she tried to comprehend the news. Would things ever feel "normal" again? How would this affect her family as a whole? Would the diagnosis affect friendships? What did this mean for their finances? Would Truett be able to juggle the load of type 1 when he was on his own? It felt like such earth-shattering news, and she wondered if things would ever feel settled again. We talked about embracing where God had all of us, and this new type 1 life, and totally trusting God, knowing he had a special plan for Truett's life.

Grandbabies Truett, Ellis, Anna, Vega, Collins and Grant 2020

Truett turned six years old in 2019, and for the most part, he leads a very normal life as a little boy in kindergarten. He plays baseball and soccer, swims on the swim team, has play dates with friends, and enjoys being with his family. It has taken years of reframing and processing to get there for them, but they have all adjusted quite well to the news that forever changed his life four years ago. God is already using Truett and his parents to touch the lives of many with their overcoming story, and I have no doubt they will continue to do so in the years to come.

In September 2017, our family received a new addition. Grant Robert Maxwell arrived five weeks early. Shortly after he was born, the doctor came into my daughter-in-law's hospital room and stated that they had noticed some signs of Down syndrome in the baby and wanted to do further testing.

This was a big surprise and sudden jolt to all of us, especially his parents, as there had been numerous tests, sonograms, etc. and nothing in her pregnancy indicated this diagnosis. Tests confirmed that Grant had Trisomy 21, also known as Down syndrome.

My daughter-in-law said the news was so shocking; she could not comprehend what had just been told to her by the doctor. She did not know much about the diagnosis and said it felt like she had been handed a prison sentence at first. In reality, it was the beginning of grieving the idea of the little boy she thought she was having and going to be raising. She later stated that she realized she was just grieving the idea of a particular child who never really existed. Sometimes, we can grieve ideas or expectations, not just a particular person.

Grant turned two years old in September of 2019 and is a delight to our family. His mom and dad have done an exceptional job of embracing the challenges and celebrating the blessings that go with raising a child with special needs.

Kathleen's oldest son, Austin and his wife Laura, Collins and Grant

In all these diagnoses, the grief process was beginning. The process of letting go of dreams, ideas, and expectations needed to happen. Embracing the new reality and finding a rhythm for life could then begin. Fortunately, the grief my children went through with losing their dad prepared them in many ways for other life challenges.

Loss of Virginity, Abuse, or Molestation

In my years of ministry, especially when I was director of the Christian Women's Job Corps of Kerr County, I had numerous women that came into my office and began a conversation something like this: "I have never told anyone this, but I was raped, molested, or abused."

For the first time in the lives of these women, they felt safe and were in a place they could admit some of the deep, traumatic, and hurtful things they had been through in life. One of my daily prayers for my clients was for God to heal the broken pieces of their hearts, and it was my honor to be a part of their process.

When they began to process their abuse, that was when sorrow set in.

In ministering to them, my constant prayer was for healing of their broken heart. I found it was important to encourage them to grieve what had been stolen from them and begin the process of forgiveness and letting go. God could then restore their dignity and value.

I also noticed that many of the women struggled with depression due to the suppressed grief and trauma they had experienced. Letting go was important in order for them to move on in many areas of their lives.

Facing the reality that something valuable had been taken from them, grabbing hold of the grace of God, and choosing to forgive their offender began the process. For many, it was the first time they had actually shed tears over their situation. It is important in the grieving process that they see God as a God of hope and restoration.

Grief and Loss of a Marriage or Relationship or Community of People

My marriage to my late husband went through some rough waters. During that time, there was real sadness in my heart. One day, I was visiting with a dear friend about the situation, and she said some powerful words that opened my eyes.

She said, "Kathleen, you are grieving the marriage you thought you had." She was right, and it was one of my first understandings of the grief process.

I began to read about grief during that time, and sure enough, I was in a process of letting go of the marriage I thought I had.

The great news is after much letting go of the marriage I thought I had, God restored our relationship and our marriage became much better than it had ever been.

I have never been divorced but have visited and ministered to many people that have been divorced. Divorce is the death of a relationship and the loss of a dream for many. Some begin the process when the marriage falls apart. For others, the reality sets in when the divorce is final. Letting go is crucial to moving forward and grief is part of the healing of the heart.

Also grief is present for the children of those that divorce. Their family is dramatically changed. When a divorce takes place, it is important to realize that children, adult children, are thrust into the grief process, whether they like it or not. It is imperative that we allow them to grieve their loss and express their sorrow. Holidays are never the same, as well as special events in their lives. Even though the child may be mature enough to understand the divorce and think it is good, their hearts need healing. Many things are now different for a person whose parents divorce.

I remember losing a dear friend due to a misunderstanding. It came at a time not long after I lost my husband. It was another loss for me at a time I was already grieving. I missed the frequent communication and fun we had experienced. I missed laughing with my friend and sharing life with her.

I was sad that there was loss of relationship and realized that she too was in her own grief over difficult things in her life.

Oftentimes, if people have not experienced a grief in their own life, they have no comprehension or real compassion for those that are grieving. This can often lead to judgement and misunderstandings, which are added difficulties to someone in grief.

I had to walk through the steps of grief and forgiveness in this loss. The relationship has begun to heal, and I love watching God redeem things.

In the grief process, we get the opportunity to get to know God in a more intimate way and develop a relationship with the Comforter. When we let go, we open the door to God's healing and restoration.

In visiting with widows and widowers, many have expressed loss of relationship with some family and extended family members, as the process of probating the will begins. This is extremely difficult, as it compounds the grief everyone is already experiencing. Grief emotions are magnified in situations like this and it is another trauma when the family relationship cannot be repaired or the relationship ends.

Chapter 5

Stages of Grief

(Please note that everyone does not go through the stages in the same order. We may stay in one stage longer than another depending on the loss. Each grief can be different.)

Shock

Learning that we have lost someone dear to us is oftentimes very hard to wrap our mind and emotions around, even when the death is expected.

With my late husband Joe, my mom and dad, I knew their death was near, as they were all three on hospice care, and physical signs were apparent that death was near. There was a cushion I felt wrapped around me for about the first six weeks after all of them were gone.

There was so much to do with the memorial services, family in town, friends around, and many tasks. There was also a deep longing in me to get back to work, as it was something normal. I just wanted something to be normal. The shock of their deaths helped me slowly face the reality of the fact that they were gone from this earth and life would forever be different.

In 1997, I lost a baby suddenly. When the doctor told me the baby was gone, I was all alone in the room, and my three children were in the waiting room. It was a sudden jolt to my mind, emotions, and body; however, all I could think about was how I was going to tell my kids there was not going to be a new addition to the family. Shock helped me quickly move to protective mode of the children I had, giving me a cushion, so I could deal with the reality. I also felt numb, like I was moving in quicksand, slowly through the motions of life.

When a death or loss happens unexpectedly or suddenly, the shock is significant. When my daughter-in-law suddenly lost her father due to a heart issue, she described the news as something her mind grasps; however, her heart was trying desperately to wrap around the news that her dad would be gone forever in her life. She was going through the motions of quickly getting back to Texas, but all along thinking, *What can I do to fix this?*

Shock oftentimes provides a special ability to function, and it oftentimes appears as "things are all right."

I have visited with a number of widows about suddenly losing their husbands. One said her body was in such shock, and her mind did not want to absorb it or believe the loss had happened. She said it was like she had been punched in the stomach and could not breathe. She stated the denial hit fast, and she didn't want to face the reality, yet she had to call her children and tell them their dad was gone. When she would wake up in the mornings following his death, she would wake up crying and her body would literally ache as she saw her new reality.

Another widow I visited with, talked about how she had a sudden heart attack right after she suddenly discovered her husband died. Shock can affect people differently. The news of her husband's death was so overwhelming that there were physical effects of his death.

I think God provided shock for us to give our hearts and minds time to move to the next stage of grief. I also found there was a great grace in this time, a gift from the God of comfort, as there is only so much you can handle.

Denial

Oftentimes, it is easier to pretend a traumatic event has not really happened. We really do not want the truth to be the truth. We do not really want to face the facts or where we are in life. Perhaps "this" really has not happened. We cling to a false, preferable reality.

When I suddenly lost the baby, my tummy did not automatically go back to its original state. I still wanted to wear maternity clothes as I really still wanted to be pregnant. In the early days, I cognitively knew I was not expecting; however, it was easier to be in denial for a little while than face the reality.

During my mom's battle with Churg-Strauss syndrome, I watched my dad stay in denial for years about her illness. The disease she had attacked her brain and caused her to lose some cognitive ability. The doctor had told us that the brain damage was irreversible. We were praying and believing God to touch her. We had faith, even though we were watching her slowly slip away.

There were days when she was bright eyed, funny, and could talk about things in her past. On those days, the good days, he would think she was getting better and try to tell me she was getting well, almost as if he forgot, what yesterday was like.

Kathleen and her parents Landon and Mary Belle

It was hard for all of us to believe this was happening to our sweet mother, that she might not ever be the same, that her condition would not get much better and could get worse.

I would watch my dad rehearse with my mom, as we drove to see the neurologist, the basic questions the doctor was going to ask. The conversation went something like this.

"Now, Mary, this month is May and today is May 9. The year is 2007. Our president is George Bush."

His denial was easier than facing the possibility that his trophy wife was not going to bounce back and be the woman he married.

The buffer shock provides, and the moments or days of denial are God's provision, as oftentimes, people are not really ready to deal with the heartache they are experiencing.

Unfortunately, I have witnessed some people stay in the denial stage for years, afraid the pain of embracing the reality, will be too much for them to bear.

Little do they realize, staying in the denial stage too long, can keep them stuck and from moving forward in their life.

In my life, God was right beside me, ready to help me embrace the pain and accept the reality that someone I loved dearly was gone. Oftentimes, people can miss the comfort and the courage He provides in our time of need, because they are too busy blaming him for their crisis or trying to protect themselves from the pain by staying in denial.

For many years of my life, when something went wrong or not like I thought it should, I blamed God, felt like He had abandoned or forgotten me. I totally missed that He was right beside me, waiting for me to accept his help, his tender mercy, and help me overcome whatever I was facing.

God promises to always be with us. Psalms 73:23 (NIV) states, "Nevertheless, I will be with you, I hold you by the right hand."

This has been one of my favorite life scriptures and has brought me great comfort.

Anger

One day, I was standing in my kitchen and dealing with some financial issues that my late husband normally took care of. I was thinking deeply about some decisions, and I felt inadequate in making these decisions alone.

All of a sudden, a wave of anger washed over me. I was mad! I was mad that Joe left me. I was mad that I was having to deal with issues he dealt with. I was mad at the world!

I picked up the pen I was writing with and threw it across the room. Then I picked up something else close by and threw it too, and it broke. Typically, I am easy going and optimistic about life in general. What on earth had come over me? I had never lost control of my emotions and thrown something before.

I sat down and began sobbing, releasing the emotions I did not know were inside of me. What was wrong with me? This was not like me.

44

It was the anger stage of grief that snuck up on me and blindsided me.

In the days ahead, there would be moments of anger that would come out of nowhere. They were part of my grief process and gave me an opportunity to embrace the reality of where I was in life and partner with the grief process.

I have also seen others in the anger stage of grief be angry with themselves for not doing certain things. They did not realize someone they love would be gone and they are angry because of regrets.

Oftentimes, we simply do not want to be where we are in life for multiple reasons, and this makes us angry.

Our anger is usually rooted in one of two things, fear or unforgiveness.

When I find myself angry, I usually step back and examine my heart. Am I afraid of something? Has someone hurt me, and it is trapped in my subconscious, and I need to deal with it? *Who do I need to forgive? A person, God, myself?*

If we do not embrace and deal with our anger, it can keep us from moving forward in the grief process. Sometimes, I knew I needed to forgive; I just was not ready. God loves the honesty of our heart and praying a simple prayer.

> *"Lord, help my heart to be ready and willing to forgive,"* is a good place to start the process.

Asking yourself the above simple questions and dealing with them are keys to freedom.

Forgiveness is also a choice and an act of our will.

For years, I operated from the perspective that I would forgive when I felt like it. Unfortunately, that kept me stuck for years. When I realized that I could choose to forgive and ask God to change my heart, it was so liberating!

My new prayer became, "God, I choose as an act of my will to forgive _____. I choose to forgive because you said so. Please change my heart."

God has been so faithful to answer that prayer and set me free and keep me moving in the grief process.

We forgive because God said so numerous times in scripture. We forgive, so we will be forgiven. We forgive as an act of obedience and so we can move forward in our lives.

Matthew 6:14–15 (NIV) states, "For *if you* forgive men when they sin against you, your heavenly Father will also forgive you. But **if you** do not forgive men their sins, your Father will not forgive your sins."

We all need forgiveness of our sins. Even though my late husband did not sin in dying and leaving me, his death caused hurt and pain to my heart. I had to forgive him for leaving me to deal with many things alone. The process to freedom is still the same.

Fear is a big part of anger. In grief, anger can be rooted in being afraid of being alone, afraid no one will love me now, afraid it will always hurt this bad, afraid we will be sad forever and never laugh or experience joy. These are all things to wrestle with, but again, our feelings can lie to us, and fear is not from God.

2 Timothy 1:7 (KJV) tells us, "For *God* hath *not given us* the *spirit of fear*; but *of* power, and *of* love, and *of a* sound mind." I discovered several things from this scripture. Fear does not come from God, and God gives us power to overcome, promises love, and will give us a sound mind. I had to tell fear to leave; I did not want to listen to it. It was not my friend.

I challenge you when you find yourself angry in any situation, ask God what you might be afraid of or who you need to forgive. Those are keys to walking out of anger and to begin to thrive in life.

I have also found that when I am afraid of anything, I need God to touch my heart and ask Him to love me in that place. I need a greater revelation of His perfect, unconditional love for me.

I pray a simple prayer of, "Lord, I realize I have some fear in this area and need you to love me in this place in my heart."

When I stop and let Him love me in the place I feel vulnerable, healing comes.

Forgiveness and Grief

Forgiveness is a big part of moving forward after a loss. There are many aspects of forgiveness, and in my own life, it has been a process of forgiving people, myself, and God in order to move forward. This may sound funny since the person that died might not have had a choice in their death. However, there might have been other choices they could have made that could have resulted in a different outcome.

All of these were huge in healing my heart and moving forward to wholeness. *The key is to choose to forgive when you realize you need to and ask God to heal your heart.*

To forgive means to cancel or pardon a debt, to stop feeling angry or resentful of someone for an offense or loss. Forgiveness puts us in control, and grief can often make us feel out of control.

Also, realize that forgiving and healing of the heart are two different things. Forgiveness begins the process of healing, just like surgery can begin to deal with a physical issue and healing from the surgery can take time. I have had several surgeries in my lifetime, and surgery was usually a few hours; however, the weeks of healing and getting back to my normal self took time.

Sometime after I lost my baby, something triggered my grief and anger emerged. I realized that I needed to forgive God for letting me lose the baby. I realized I was mad at Him because I wanted this child and loved it, even though it was not born. We prayed for healing when my miscarriage began, and my prayers were not answered the way I wanted them to be answered. I was disappointed.

Focusing on disappointments can lead us to unforgiveness, which leads to anger.

My prayer went something like this, "God, I know you are perfect, and your ways are perfect, but I am mad at you that this baby did not make it. I admit my anger and choose as an act of my will to forgive you." I needed to vocalize my feelings in order to deal with them.

God meets us right where we are and loves us. We can be real with Him and pour out the anguish that is in our hearts. He knows about it anyway.

Several years into my marriage to Stephen, we were having a conversation and I felt like he was not listening to what I was saying about a situation. I felt like I was right, and all of a sudden, I got angry at him. As I prayed about the situation and asked God why I had responded like I did, I felt like He showed me my response to my husband was rooted in my past. For years, I had asked Joe to wear sunscreen, and he did not. His cancer was related to sun exposure. I realized I needed to forgive Joe not listening to me about sunscreen.

If you find yourself not responding like you normally would, even years after your loss, consider forgiveness. Ask God to show you if your present response is linked in any way to your loss or anyone you need to forgive. God loves relationship with us, and as you ask Him and seek Him, I know He will show you, if not immediately, eventually.

Another time in my life, I realized that I needed to forgive people for not understanding and judging me in grief. Our society, especially those that have never been through a significant loss, can easily judge and not understand those that are grieving. Have you ever felt like people have not understood your loss and pain? Maybe you need to forgive them.

I encourage you to take time to reflect on this chapter, as it is a big key in moving forward in your grief. As I stated, even years after I lost my husband and most of my grieving was over, there were still those little things that popped up, and I needed to deal with them. Have some real conversations with God and pour out your heart to Him. Get what is inside of you out, and ask for His healing touch. He loves relationship with us.

Sorrow Sets In

As the days and months go by, the heart needs to admit that it is disappointed or sad that it misses someone or something that was dear to their heart. Sorrow begins to set in. Our heart hurts. This is the real tough part of grief.

Each grieving person has to go through the pain to heal. No one is exempt. You cannot go around it and heal. Embrace the sorrow your heart feels and realize that as you meet it head on, you will move through the process quicker.

I do not know many people that like to be in a position where their heart hurts. Oftentimes, people pretend it does not hurt, and this is not healthy.

There is risk in loving and when you love deeply, you can get hurt, but the alternative is a hard heart.

If we are not feeling, we are not really living. It is okay to embrace the sorrow your heart feels and realize this is part of the grief process.

During this time, I would wake up and feel like my life was over. Cognitively, I knew that was not true, and I had a lot to live for. I was young, had three beautiful children, grandchildren to look forward to, I had great friends and knew God had plans for my life; however, my heart was sad, lonely, and it was a time of wrestling with my feelings.

Let me stress the word, *wrestle*. Our mind can know something to be true; however, there is the battle that rages with our feelings, and our feelings can lie to us. Each of us has a choice in these situations, to live in the truth of God's word or live in our feelings.

I would wake up in the morning but wanted to lay in bed and cry. *Why go on? I might not ever laugh again; my life is over*, were some of the thoughts I struggled with.

I knew and remembered the scriptures like Jeremiah 29:11 (NIV), "For I know the plans I have for you," declares the Lord, "plans to prosper you and not to harm you, plans to give you hope and a future." Again cognitively, I knew this was truth; however, it was not what my feelings were telling me. I had to wrestle with them, embrace the pain and sorrow, and keep walking through the valley of the shadow of death. There was life ahead for me; it just did not feel like it.

During this time, fear can also be a feeling we contend with. I had a good friend call me a few months after her mother died. The conversation began with, "Kathleen, I don't know what is wrong with me. I am not a fearful person, but all of a sudden, there are irrational fears I am struggling with. Can you pray for me?"

As we visited and she shared her heart, I was able to see that the sorrow had set in, and the fear she was contending with was simply part of the grief process.

She was embracing her loss. Her heart was tender. She did not have to be afraid of the future, and recognizing her fears were irrational was a huge step. I prayed for peace and comfort of the Holy Spirit to pour over her and bring healing.

When in the sorrow stage of grief in my life, one of the scriptures I held on to was Proverbs 31:25 (NIV), which talks about a godly woman. It states, "She is clothed with strength and dignity;

she can laugh at the days to come." Although this passage refers to a godly woman, I certainly think this scripture applies to men too.

Oftentimes, when we lose someone or something we love, we are faced with the reality that no matter how much we try to control and keep things in order in our lives, there are many things beyond us.

Death is a part of life.

We have no guarantees of tomorrow, and life is short. Somehow the sorrow stage of grief highlights these statements and facts of life.

As difficult as the sorrow stage of grief is, always remember it is not God's heart for you to stay here but keep moving through the process.

My simple prayer during this time was, *"God, this hurts. Heal my broken heart and keep me moving through the process."* God was faithful to answer this prayer

We Begin to Let Go

Letting go is a major part of grief and very important. We must say goodbye to the person or season to move on. This does not mean we say goodbye to the good memories; those are our treasures to carry in our heart forever. As we let go, the bad or traumatic memories begin to fade, and for me, didn't have the sting they once did.

Letting go may not sound fun, but when our loss has been great, our loved one deserves to be honored with goodbyes. This is necessary to move forward, otherwise, we will stay stuck, sad, depressed, and that is not what God has for us.

Jesus said in John 10:10 (NIV), "I have come that they may have life, and have it to the full." God has an abundant life ahead for anyone grieving. I clung to this scripture during the letting go process.

Writing a letter to say goodbye to the person that has died or the season of life you will not experience is a great way to honor what you have lost. This is not necessarily a letter that anyone but you, sees. Putting something on paper helps us realize what we are really feeling. It is putting our feelings into tangible words and pouring out our heart.

There are many ways to let go. When my grandfather died, I struggled, as it was one of my first losses. I remember one day eating something and then thinking, *I am not even hungry*. It was then I realized I was "feeding" my pain and needed to let go. I sat down that day and wrote my grandfather a long letter, telling him what he meant to me, how he had impacted my life, how much I loved and missed him. I am not going to lie; it was gut-wrenching; however, I felt so much better after putting on paper what I needed to say.

I never showed anyone the letter. It was my letter to him and a way of letting go and honoring his life.

After my miscarriage, I penned a letter to the baby, honoring the life I had lost. The letter consisted of how much I was looking forward to this little life, the dreams I had for her in our family, and telling her goodbye. I am a person that loves deeply, so letting go is not the easiest thing for me. My letter was written to this baby as if I were talking to the child, sharing my dreams and then saying good-bye to the life I would never hold.

The major key I learned in the letting-go time was asking God each morning, "God, what do I need to let go of today?"

During these days, there were many mixed emotions. There was a part of me that was tired of the heartache and sorrow and was ready for something different. There were days I felt like I did not want to let go of anymore; however, the more I let go of, the more I could get on with my new life. There were also days, I felt like I needed a break from letting go. It was a fine line, and the key for me was one day at a time and one step at a time.

Embracing the pain and sorrow that is in our heart can be challenging but necessary to move on. I remember it was a hallmark day when I had my first day of not crying after losing my husband. Honestly, I did not think a person could cry that much. Four months after Joe was gone, I wrote in my journal, "Today was the first day I did not cry. It was a good day. The pain seems less, I am healing."

These days were exhausting, and I had to learn to be patient with myself.

Embracing the pain gives us an opportunity to grow and move in a positive direction. I have discovered the process makes you rich.

In the natural, no one gets new life without pain. Ask any woman that has given birth, it did not come without pain. When I could look at the grief as something with purpose, to bring me to a new life, it helped. I did not like embracing the pain and letting go; however, it had purpose. It was birthing my new life.

There were some times when I was in my lonely house, I would literally scream. "Why did you leave me? I do not like living alone!" It was okay. Just as it would be all right for a woman to scream in pain during childbirth. I was birthing a new life and it hurt.

There were many entries in my journal of writing letters to Joe and processing my grief. There was something about putting my thoughts and feelings on paper that helped let go.

When grieving my late husband, this was a daily process as I had much to let go of. Letting go of all his clothes, possessions, our dreams together, the way it was supposed to be, and many other things.

Letting go of thirty-three years with someone takes time. If I looked at *all* I needed to let go of, it was overwhelming. Somehow, when I looked at only what I needed to let go of each day, it was an easier pill to swallow. I had to look at what needed to be let go of that day.

Joe and I had married young and had our first child eighteen months later. We always talked about when the kids were gone, we would have our time to travel and our second honeymoon. Our youngest had just started college when he was diagnosed with cancer. A big loss I had to release, was our dream of what this season of life would look like. It was a huge letting go because we had talked of the empty nest fondly for years.

One day, I had to vocalize it and said, "God, I let go of all my dreams of travel, second honeymoon, and the golden years." The words were difficult to get out of my mouth, but I said them through the tears. I felt that if I let go of them, it was dishonoring, or I might not ever travel again. That was not true, but it was how I felt. I was embracing the pain. I gave the pain to God. He was big enough to carry it; I was not.

I felt God say, "Kathleen, I will give you new dreams and adventures." I had to let go of *my* dream, so God could give me new ones and a new life.

Each time I let go of something, my heart began to heal a little more. Letting go finally became my friend and my key to moving forward.

Ten years have passed since I said those words. I remarried three years after my husband died, and my new husband, Stephen and I have traveled many places in the world. I have learned to do many new things, like quail hunt, dove hunt, fishing, and dancing, just to name a few. I now have a new life and it is a good one.

Our family at our wedding 2012

Kathleen and Stephen in west Texas

Dove hunting in Argentina

Keys to Letting Go and Ways to Say Goodbye

- *Crying and pouring your heart out to God. Let the tears roll alone and when in public. Tears are a natural release of your grief. They are healing and you never have to apologize for them.*

- *Write a letter to yourself, God or a person or season of life. Journaling is a great way to process your feelings.*

- *Choose to forgive. You may need to forgive the person for dying and leaving you, forgive a spouse for leaving the marriage, forgive God, forgive the person that took their life. Forgiveness keeps our heart soft. Pray, "God, I choose as an act of my will to forgive. Change my heart and heal it."*

- *Admit when your heart hurts. My prayer looked something like this, "Lord, this still hurts, I open my heart to you, please heal me." This is not denying or medicating our pain. It is embracing it.*

This process is sometimes like surgery. At times in life, we have to get a surgery in order to heal. We need surgery to heal, and healing takes time and work.

It takes time to process and accept our loss. Oftentimes, the heart wants to resist or fight against the acceptance of the loss.

Somehow, this can feel like we are saying the loss is okay, a positive thing, when in reality, we see it as a big negative in our lives.

Acceptance is the realization and embracing of the fact that the event or loss has happened, and our life will forever be different.

It does not mean we have to like the change. It does mean we begin to look for the positive things that can come into our lives, and we begin to live life again.

This can come in stages. Acceptance helps the heart move forward. Acceptance does not mean we forget; it just means our heart comes to the realization that things will not be the same.

I remember when I began accepting my husband's death and began dating again. One of my children said this about the man I was seeing, "Mom, he is not like dad. He is different."

My reply was, "Yes, this man is different. Your dad is gone and is not coming back. I am not looking for someone just like him. He's gone."

I will admit, at first, I did look for someone like Joe. One day, I had to accept the fact that he was gone, and I would drive myself crazy trying to "find" him again. I swallowed the pill of acceptance.

Chapter 6

Challenges of Grief

One of the challenges of grief is, it is exhausting. I am a high energy person, and I found in my seasons of grief, they were exhausting and took a great deal of energy. I had to learn to pace myself and not over commit to things. Tasks I was normally able to do with ease were much harder and took more time. Grief zapped my energy.

People that have not been through grief, will probably not understand you and judge you. You cannot fault someone for not knowing what they have not personally experienced; however, their lack of sensitivity can cause distress at a time when you personally are dealing with stress and change. All of us have a desire to be understood. It is important to forgive and not sever relationship. Sometimes, healthy boundaries are good to put into place.

Grief is emotional pain and just like physical healing takes time, so does emotional healing. It took me two years to feel like myself again physically and emotionally after losing my husband.

Grief can feel like anxiety or trigger anxiety. When we lose something or someone dear to us, we are faced with the reality that we are not in control of anything. This reality can make you feel anxious at times. I have a friend that is a very strong individual; however, after losing one of her parents, she called one day asking for prayer. As I listened to her, it became evident that the grief had arrived, and this made her feel anxious which was unusual for her. We prayed, discussed processing grief, and she later said it was very helpful to understand why she was feeling anxious. Oftentimes, panic attacks can occur in seasons of grief. Let me encourage you if this happens, let the tears roll and ask God to comfort you and settle your heart. I have only had one panic attack in my life, and it happened about six months into my grief journey. I was traveling alone and in another state. All of a sudden, this wave of panic hit me. I was undone and alone. I was not sure what to do and almost felt like I needed to call 911. I threw myself on the bed and turned on some Christian worship music and let the comforting words of God's faithfulness, wash over me. After about thirty minutes of sobbing and listening to the music, I felt okay.

Focusing on "why" can keep you from moving forward.

It is easy to focus on the "why" question. Why did this happen to me, why now, etc.; however, the why question can keep us stuck. There are just things here on earth that we will not understand. Focusing on why, replaying things in your mind that if you had done something different, you would not be in this place, struggling with feelings of guilt, will keep you immobile in the grief process. Focus on *what*. For me, asking God what He wanted to work in me and out of me, instead of asking why, kept me moving through the grief process.

Chapter 7

Important Things to Know About Grief

Grief is a process and cannot be rushed. Each grief experience is a little different, and some things take longer than others to process. Do not rush the process. I have had friends that have lost their mother or father. Their parent lived in another city, not the same town as they did. They only saw their parent a few times a year. Their grief was much different than mine, as my parents lived in my town, and I was daily involved with their lives and care for years. I had friends share that they missed their parents, but it was not as much of a loss because they were not part of their daily routine.

When someone has surgery, they may take out the cancer, do a knee replacement, etc. but the person doesn't walk out of the hospital healed. The healing has begun and takes time. It is the same way with grief. *The bigger the loss in your life, the longer the process. Partner with the process.*

Honor the pain, but don't live in it. Some people and cultures idolize a person that has died. God does not intend for us to live in grief. Jesus came so we could have abundant life. Psalms 23:4 (KJV) says, "Yea, though I walk *through* the valley of the shadow of death, I will fear no evil: for you are with me; thy rod and thy staff, they comfort me." God's intention is stated in this verse. He is with us and wants us to go *through* this valley, not stay there. When I first read this passage, it was of great comfort to me to discover, grief was not the destination and was like a town that I would just drive through.

The greater the love/relationship and investment in your life, the longer the process takes. My late husband and I had a very integrated life. We did pretty much everything together and had a strong marriage when he died. I have had several other widows that knew us make the statement that they did not have a great relationship with their husband, lived separate lives, and had grown apart before their loss. They stated they wished they had had the kind of relationship we shared and also said things changed for them with the loss, however, they dealt more with regret of not having the marriage they wished they had had.

The important thing with grief is to keep moving through it. My constant prayer during grief has always been, "God, keep me moving *through* the stages of grief. I do not want to get stuck." It is okay to take a break and rest in the process, but when pain surfaces, deal with it, do not stuff it. This will keep you moving through it. Also, take honest periodic inventory of where you are in the process and keep the goal to move along.

If grief is not dealt with initially, it will resurface. I have seen in my own life and in many others, the defense mechanism of procrastination to avoid grief and dealing with our emotions of the loss. In the earlier years of my life, I did not understand the process or importance; therefore, I stuffed much of my pain, only to find out it would resurface later in my life.

When my husband died, my youngest son was a freshman at The University of Texas and was studying to be a petroleum engineer. I realized that with the loss of his father and his academic load, he might not have the capacity to grieve for a while. He was stepping into manhood without his dad, had a tough major, and knew finances were tight. It wasn't until about four years later, he came to me and said, "Mom, I don't think I have ever really grieved losing dad." I agreed and prayed with him, and he began his own journey of dealing with his loss.

Kathleen, widowed and youngest son Price

Our feelings can lie to us in times of grief. When dealing with grief, it is important to process our feelings, but also ask God to reveal truth to us. I felt like my life was over after losing my husband. There were days I did not want to go on because it seemed too hard. The truth was life as I knew it had forever changed. The life with Joe was gone; however, there was still much for me to live for. God had a plan for my life, and He was right in the middle of it. My constant prayer was "God reveal truth in any area I have believed a lie about myself and my life." God was faithful to show me and lead me and this is still one of my favorite prayers in many different areas of life.

The beauty of grief is that it can work things into us and out of us. When we partner with grief, embrace it as a friend, beauty can come into our lives. I am a much different woman than I was before losing my husband and parents. I did not want to waste the pain I was experiencing and wanted it to change me and shape me to become more like Christ. I am much more compassionate and kinder than I was years ago. I also have a confidence that I never had before because I have had to look death in the face, and I have seen God's faithfulness to me in the valleys of life.

I have seen other widows and widowers that have looked at their grief as a tool to shape them, and conversely, I have seen other widows and widowers that looked at their grief negatively and have stayed stuck in life and have not become better people. Grief is a tool that can work well when we pick it up and use it to our advantage.

Grief will come like waves in the ocean. Do not be disillusioned that you are not making progress when one hits. One of the crazy things about grief is it can sneak up behind you and hit you like a wave. For years, we went to the beach. I loved being in the water and riding the waves. When I faced the shore and had my back to the waves, they would hit me from behind and knock me over, leaving me gasping for breath and trying to get my feet back under me. That is exactly how grief hits. You can be fine one day or moment, loving life and enjoying yourself, and all of a sudden, a wave of grief hits, leaving you wondering what happened and gasping for breath and in tears.

One day, I remember thinking that I was finally getting back to being myself and beginning to get a little healing for my heart. A few hours later, I saw something that I had seen numerous times, but this time, I was in tears because of the painful reminder of my loss. I remember thinking I really had not made any progress in my grief and felt defeated. This was not true. I was making progress. Waves of grief can hit out of nowhere. Get back up, take a deep breath, and realize this is just part of the process. Embrace the wave. Admit that the loss still hurts but get back to enjoying life and know another wave will come and it is okay.

Grief is a time of transition. The purpose of transition is to move us from one place to another. Transition is defined as the process or a period of changing from one state or condition to another. Ask any woman that has gone through the process of giving birth naturally, and I am sure she will tell you it hurt. I had all three of my children naturally.

With my firstborn, when I was in the transition phase, it was the most difficult for me. I thought I was going to die, and I was not sure I cared! In the birth process, a woman moves from being in labor, to beginning to push the new life into the world.

Grief is the same way. Life is not the same. Something new is coming in our life, but oftentimes, this does not occur without pain. It is very important to remember that this is a season, just a part of your life. You must keep your focus on the fact that this process will bring you to a new place and new life because it is easy to believe the sorrow you feel, will be like this forever.

There are times, ten years down the road, I still miss my late husband, but I do not feel the intense sorrow I did during the first few years after losing him. The grief I experienced gave birth to a new and confident woman, new ministry opportunities, a new husband, and lots of adventure.

No grief experience is exactly the same. I have been through numerous grief experiences in my life, and each was a little different in length, intensity, and processing. Realize that your journey might look a little different than someone else's loss. Different is not wrong, it is just different.

I have a good friend that lost her husband suddenly, and she still had a child at home. Although we were the same age and had both lost our husbands, our grief experiences were different. I had more time to process, living alone, and did not have some of the responsibilities and demands on my life that she had raising a teenager. We cannot compare ourselves to others. We must keep moving forward in our own grief journey.

Kathleen and daughter Mallory

My daughter got married nine months after her dad died. She was busy planning a wedding, being a wife, and adjusting to life in a new city. A few years later, she realized she needed to work through some things in her grief process and sought out a professional counselor. She simply had not had the time and capacity to process right after her dad passed away.

You, not others, are responsible for your healing. Each of us is responsible for our own journey. When my late husband and I had some problems in our marriage, we went through a rough five years. There was much sorrow in my heart. At first, I looked to my husband to heal my broken heart. I finally realized, in this grief, I had to be responsible for my journey and could not look to someone else, other than God, to heal my heart. Often, those around us have broken hearts and their own issues and pain they are dealing with.

Trying to put your healing on others is not fair to them. Your grief journey is your own. After I lost my husband, I could not look to my kids to heal me. They had their own lives, jobs, family, etc. and had also lost their father. They were dealing with a lot. We had raised our children to be independent, self-sufficient, and trained them to seek God. I wanted them to flourish in life, and it was not their responsibility to heal *my* broken heart. It was my responsibility to keep giving my broken heart to God and walk with Him as he healed me.

Kathleen and three children, Austin, Price and Mallory at Price's wedding

It is easy to try to put responsibility on someone else when you are hurting. When we look to others to heal us, it is like trying to grab ahold of someone when you are drowning. A lifesaving device will be much better in getting us to safety than trying to depend on others. That lifesaving device is Jesus. He understands our pain and sorrow and most of the time, others will not and are wrapped up in their own world.

One word of caution, grief can make you very self-centered. The pain of grief is real; however, few people like being around someone that thinks the world should revolve around their pain, needs, and world. People that are self-centered are difficult to be around and are not fun to be around.

I began to see this in myself at times and did not like what I saw. I looked to God to help me and change me and took responsibility for my healing. I have seen self-centeredness in other grieving people. It manifests in wanting plans to change and revolve around their need, only talking about themselves, not asking questions of others in conversations and looking to others to fix them. Only God can bring healing and each of us needs to be responsible for our own journey.

I am a different person, a better person, because of what I learned in my journey with grief and looking to God, not others, in my pain. I know from personal experience, only God can heal broken hearts.

Grief can exaggerate fear. One of the things it is important to realize is grief makes fear look even bigger than ever before. I had overcome a lot of fears in my life, but all of a sudden after losing Joe, I battled fear like never before.

Fear is not your friend and is a robber of peace. Our emotions are on high alert after losing someone or something we loved. Realizing this and understanding the fact that our emotions are being tossed around can help one find peace in their heart quicker.

We have a God-given right to walk in peace in any situation in life. When fear shows up on your doorstep, you can either open the door and let it ransack your life or slam the door in its face. You and you alone get to choose.

Jesus said in John 14:27 (NIV), *"Peace I leave with you; my peace I give you. I do not give to you as the world gives. Do not let your hearts be troubled and do not be afraid."* If someone gives you a present, you can either open it up and enjoy it or leave it in the package. When I grasp that concept, it opened a door for many peaceful days.

I remember one day when Joe and I were at MD Anderson and had just received some devastating news about his diagnosis. I excused myself and went to the bathroom and looked at myself in the mirror. I had to preach to myself and I said, "Kathleen, you will walk in peace." I took a deep breath and walked out of the ladies' room and felt much better. That simple declaration helped tremendously and brought my heart to a state of peace.

Anniversaries, special days, places, and holidays can often trigger grief. Somehow, our subconsciousness remembers. It can be the wedding anniversary or birthday of someone you lost. It can be the day you were diagnosed with cancer. The anniversary of the day someone you loved died or any other monumental day in your life. It can also be birthdays, places that were special to you and/or the person. It can also be the days leading up to the anniversary too. All these things and others can trigger grief and cause another wave to come crashing over us.

Prior to anniversaries as well as on the anniversary itself, you may not sleep as well, because subconsciously, your heart remembers that day. I also remember after losing my grandfather, around the anniversary of his death, I found myself eating one day in the middle of the day. I was not even hungry but was "feeding the pain." I was eating just to eat, not because I needed more nutrition or was even hungry.

I miscarried our baby in mid-August. Several years later, I woke up one morning and just felt down and sad. This was unlike me. As the day went on, I asked God to show me what was going on in my heart. A few hours went by, and all of a sudden, I remembered that this was August 19, the day I miscarried. It took my mind a little while to figure things out, but my heart remembered.

As I approached the anniversary of my late husband's death, the weeks prior to that day, triggered grief. I was dreading the day that forever changed my life. How would I respond on that day? What would it be like? Just knowing the anniversary of his death was approaching, made my heart unsettled. I tend to have more anticipatory grief, grief prior to the actual day. Once the anniversary day arrived, my heart was more settled, and the day was not actually that bad, but the days leading up to the anniversary were challenging as they made me feel like I had taken huge steps backwards in my grief. Although you may have made it a year or two or three down the grief path, the feelings of loss, missing what you had, and other feelings of grief, often resurface around anniversaries.

At first, I dreaded the anniversary of loss; however, now, I just see them as an opportunity to let go a little more and open my heart to God to heal. Anniversaries are also a day to reflect on how far you have come and express gratitude in your accomplishment and the accomplishments your family has made.

Thanksgiving and Christmas can be particularly difficult as these are holidays that are built around many memories. Valentine's Day, Father's Day, and Mother's Day were also challenging. So many memories surrounded those holidays and even years later, were difficult and could trigger grief that needed to be dealt with. It is totally normal for grief to come barging through the door, as an unwanted guest the weeks prior to these holidays because subconsciously, we know a special day is coming, and those we spent it with will not be around. Be aware this can happen and let the tears roll. Tears are your friend and it is important to embrace the grief. As time goes on, you will make new memories, and it will get easier, but grief just might sneak up on you years later. It is just part of the price of love.

Important Things to Remember About Grief

- *It is a process and cannot be rushed.*

- *Honor the pain, but don't live in it.*

- *The greater the love/relationship and investment in your life, the longer the process takes.*

- *The important thing with grief is to keep moving through it.*

- *If grief is not dealt with initially, it will resurface.*

- *Our feelings can lie to us in times of grief.*

- *Beauty of grief—it can work things into us and out of us.*

- *Grief will come like waves in the ocean. Do not be disillusioned that you are not making progress when one hits.*

- *Grief is a time of transition. The purpose of transition is to move us from one place to another.*

- *No grief experience is exactly the same.*

- *You, not others, are responsible for your healing.*

- *Grief can exaggerate fear.*

- *Anniversaries, special days, places, and holidays can often trigger grief.*

Chapter 8

Benefits of Grief

Grief can teach us much about ourselves and others. There are many things that grief can teach us if we let it. I learned a lot about myself, like who I was without a husband, while standing on my own two feet. I was married the majority of my adult life when my husband died. Suddenly, in the matter of one day, I was standing or at the beginning, wobbling, on my own two feet. As I journeyed alone, I discovered I was much more capable of handling things I had never handled before, than I thought.

No, I did not like where I found myself in life, but I discovered that it could be a time of learning who I was without a man. One day at a time, one step at a time, I began to see myself in a new light. I am a strong woman, but I learned I was stronger than I thought.

I also found that I knew what I wanted in life and what I did not want, even though I was in an uncertain place in life. I learned to laugh at myself too as I stumbled around trying to find my new life without my other half.

After thirty years of marriage, my late husband knew me well. He knew when I needed encouragement, when I was tired, when I needed to slow down, when I needed his touch or reminded of how much he loved me. He was good at being my balance in life. The longer we were married, the more we both realized that we were different and good for each other. We appreciated the differentness.

Now, in my unwanted state of widowhood, I no longer had any of those things that were a part of my life. Who was I without him? Was I going to make it without him giving me those things that I loved and needed?

I discovered I really was a strong woman. I could make decisions I never thought I could make. I had value and worth, even though I was no longer married, and a really fun side of me emerged.

Don't take life so seriously. When you have looked death in the face, it is easy to get caught up in the grip of life being always hard and tough. Grief takes work and is not easy. Be careful to find the treasures in each day and don't take life so seriously. Learn to laugh at yourself in your journey.

In my journeys through grief, I learned to laugh at myself. I learned to actually entertain myself, as I felt like oftentimes, I was stumbling through life. I learned to delight in the discovery of who I was becoming in the process. A whole new woman was emerging.

I have grandchildren, and it is such a delight watching their personalities develop and watching them learn to walk and talk. In my singleness and being a widow, I found God was looking at my life in much the same way, delighting in watching a new person evolve.

Grief can develop compassion in us for others. I have always said, "You don't know what you don't know." Years ago, a couple that was friends of ours lost a child. I hated it for them and did not understand some of their behavior. I now realize, I simply did not have real compassion for them because I had not encountered a loss of that magnitude.

Losing my late husband, gave me an understanding and a compassion for those that are brokenhearted. Grief softens us, can take off the rough edges, and gives us a kinder heart for those around us that are hurting or suffering.

I grew a great deal in the area of compassion for others, and it was a good thing. Grief can make us more sensitive to the needs of others, and that is always an asset.

I also learned to invest time with people whose heart had been broken. God is near to the brokenhearted and when we take moments of our day to listen and encourage others, it shapes us to be more like Christ.

Grief is a time of new beginnings, a new life and self-discovery. Grief provides us a time of starting over and doing things different. It is a time of new beginnings.

As I let go of life as I knew it with my late husband, I began to try new things that I had not done with Joe. There were no memories attached with trying new things.

One of the new things was attending swing dance lessons. A couple that were dear friends invited me to the classes with them. In this class, the women are on the outside of a circle, and the men on the inside, and you rotate partners. This was an excellent way to learn a new skill, get exercise and learn about men; what I liked and did not like. Learning new things gave me confidence to move forward even more.

I made some new friends, friends that were not a part of my old life. I began to step outside of my old box and into a new one. I made new memories.

For the first time in my life, I was not organizing my life around my husband and children. I was free to do whatever I wanted. Yes, it felt strange at first, and I felt like I had lost my purpose in life but I also quickly began to appreciate the gift of freedom to do whatever I wanted.

I frequently use this analogy when I am speaking to widows and widowers. When you lose your mate or someone that is a big part of your life, life goes on, but it is different. It is like someone cutting off your leg or a big part of your body. You are still alive, but you walk different and live in a different way. You have to adapt to a part of you being gone and you learn a new way.

Grief provides the opportunity to know God in a deeper way. I became a Christian when I was ten and grew up in church; however, during each of my journeys with grief, I grew closer to the Lord. He was the one person that never let me down, was always around to talk to, and I knew God understood my pain. He watched his son die.

Isaiah 61:1 (NIV) was a promise I clung to. It also gave me hope for the days ahead. It says, "The Spirit of the Sovereign Lord is on me, because the Lord has anointed me to preach good news to the poor. *He sent me to bind up the brokenhearted* and proclaim freedom for the captives."

The heart of God is to bind up those with a broken heart and heal them. I feel like we need to constantly bring our brokenness to God to touch.

I quickly saw that people would not always be available to comfort me and be there for me, but God was always there for me. I grew in understanding His love for me and in trusting Him. I clung to the fact that God's heart was for me and my healing.

Psalms 147:3 (NIV) states, "He heals the brokenhearted and binds up their wounds." This scripture gave me hope that my broken heart would not stay in this place forever. On the tough days, I would simply whisper a prayer, "Jesus, this hurts. Please bring another layer of healing."

Psalms 54:4 (NIV) was another scripture that helped me. It says, "Surely God is my help; the Lord is the one who sustains me." The word sustain means to uphold, strengthen, or support. I would daily look to God to uphold, strengthen, and support me in all the pain and challenges of building a new life. He was faithful as I constantly looked to Him.

Grief can help us grow in confidence and get rid of fear. No doubt there were many times in my grief journeys that I battled fear and anxiety. I remember when I was going out on my first date, a wave of anxiety made me stop in my tracks and say, "What am I doing?" I began to pray. Shortly after my prayer, a question came to mind, *Is this as bad, Kathleen, as watching tumors grow on someone you love?* No was the answer. I knew I could handle walking into the unknown with God.

That became my stabilizing question I asked myself when things seemed fearful, out of control, or I felt anxious.

Reminding ourselves of what we have been through and we survived brings confidence. It is all a matter of perspective.

Grief gives us the opportunity to practice our peace. Life here on earth is stressful, but we do not have to live stressed out lives. And real peace comes from walking with Jesus.

Losing your mate of thirty years throws you into an unknown world in many aspects. To me, everything seemed different. I was having to make decisions I had never had to make before and living life without my best friend. There were financial adjustments, and life was just different.

With so much new, I felt like I was on high alert. I quickly decided this was a great time to practice my peace, as I knew I had a God given right to walk in peace and I knew fear was not from God.

Jesus said in John 14:27 (NIV), "Peace I leave with you, my peace I give to you." I took him literally on this scripture.

When fear would try to creep in, I would take a deep breath and whisper a simple prayer and declaration.

"Fear, you are not my friend, so go. I choose as an act of my will to walk in peace." This always settled my heart.

Another scripture that really helped me was Colossians 3:15 (NIV), "Let the peace of Christ rule in your hearts, since as members of one body you were called to peace. And be thankful."

Peace is a choice. We can either let it rule in our hearts or not.

Fear and anxiety cannot coexist with peace. One of them has to go, and you and I get to choose. It took a lot of practice, but it was worth it for the confidence and peace I gained in my life. I am forever changed, and grief was my teacher.

As long as you are breathing, you can start over again. I finally realized that I had a big opportunity. Life had not turned out like I had planned; however, it was a clean slate, and I was given the opportunity to start over in many ways.

I could either become bitter or better. I could make new memories and grow into a stronger woman or sit around and miss out on life. I could get back out there and figure out how to date at fifty or sit at home and cry. It was my choice.

For me, I was not going through all this pain and not gain something from it. You have the same choice.

I began to take baby steps in many ways, and each new thing I tried, each new memory, each new relationship that was not a part of my old life, added a layer of strength. Yes, there were many days in this new and exciting phase of life that were tear-filled. But as I let grief wash over me, I would take a deep breath, wake up the next day, and try something new.

Chapter 9

What Helps and What Does Not

For friends and family of someone who
has lost a mate, parent, or child.

Be a Good Listener

If you are the friend or family of someone that has been through a great loss, you might wonder what you can do to help. Many are at a loss and desperately want to help.

Some of the things that were helpful to me and really blessed me were the people that listened and would take time to simply be with me, especially when my heart was in pain. I had lost my sounding board when I lost Joe, and I am a verbal processor. To come home and not have anyone to talk to about my day was difficult.

I had a male friend in California that frequently called me in the evenings. This was a gift to me and God's provision for a while, as he was a good listener and someone I could talk to.

People that have lost something they love want to talk about it. They want to verbally process their feelings and somehow this keeps the memories alive. *Be a good listener.* You do not have to have any answers. In fact, oftentimes, I did not want any answers. I just wanted to be heard and was lonely.

Look the person in the eye, nod, and affirm them. These things can make the grieving person feel valued and loved.

I am forever grateful for those dear friends that sat with me during the very painful times. Those that let me cry, express my heart, and took time out of their busy schedule to let me vent what I was feeling were a great asset.

I am thankful for those that would stop me in the grocery store and share a memory with me of the person I had lost. I learned many things about my late husband, my mom, and my dad from those that took time to tell me how much they had helped them, prayed with them, made them laugh, etc. These became my treasures.

Nights and weekends were also challenging. I am so grateful for friends and family that included me in their weekend activities. It always helped ease the pain of loneliness.

I frequently try to call widows or widowers in the evening, if possible, as I know the loneliness of coming home to an empty house.

Offer Specific Help

I had many people say, "Let me know what I can do to help you." There were so many things going through my mind at times, it was hard to think of what they could do. It was also difficult to call someone and ask for help. I never wanted to impose.

People that offered something specific were very helpful. One high school classmate of mine called one day and offered to bring me some wood for my fireplace. It was a winter day, and it was very cold. This was a huge gift for me and such a blessing. He stacked it neatly on my front porch and the gift of wood, something my husband would have done for me, was a tremendous help.

I had someone else call and offer to send their yardman over for a few months to help me with my yard. This was meeting a practical need, and again, something my husband always took care of.

Several months after my husband passed away, someone, I still do not know who it was, left bright yellow sunflowers on my porch. The card said something simple, "just to brighten your day." About six weeks later, another bouquet appeared again. Each time, the flowers made me smile and feel loved. They were an encouragement to me and somehow appeared at just the right time.

There was also the couple that gave me several gift certificates for massages. They were such a blessing on multiple levels as my body needed the touch and stress relief.

Finally, I sat down one day and thought of things that I could use help with. Whenever someone said the words, "let me know if I can do anything," I had a list and could send it to them or give them a few suggestions. People genuinely want to help; they just often do not know what to do.

Invite the Person for Dinner

Evenings and dinner were some of the hardest times for me in grief because for years, I had cooked dinner and planned a nice mealtime for my husband and family. After my late husband was gone, it seemed like too much work to cook for one, and there was no one to talk to and share my day.

It was very helpful to me when someone would invite me to dinner. There was a young family with three kids that was kind enough to have me over for dinner about once a month. I cannot tell you how much just the invite meant to me, as it gave me something to look forward to. I would take their kids for a ride around the block in my convertible, visit with the family, eat a great meal and always come home refreshed and feeling loved.

I was a few years down the road in my life and had wisdom to share in parenting and marriage, and they shared their life with me at a time when I needed people and something to do in the evening.

If someone has lost a parent, inviting them over for a holiday or Mother's Day or Father's Day can be very helpful. After I lost both of my parents, those first few years were particularly difficult. Inviting someone to lunch or dinner that has lost a parent will help them to see that life goes on.

Weddings are particularly difficult after losing a mate. If you are attending a wedding and know of a widow or widower that has also been invited, offer to pick them up and take them with you to the wedding. Weddings are a reminder of their own vows and what they lost, and your gift of friendship will be greatly appreciated.

Give Them Choices—Let Them Make Decisions

When death has sideswiped your life, it highlights the fact that we are not in control. Oftentimes, people that are grieving need to feel like they have some choices in life. Few people want death to take their loved one. For many, they are used to making decisions with their mate, a joint decision, and now, they are having to make them all alone, and that can be scary. Give them options. Help the grieving person take little steps and feel like they are in control of their life. Somehow, this helps the healing process. For example, if you invite them to dinner, let them choose the time, give them the choice of going out to dinner or coming over to your home for dinner, etc. Also be aware, they may at the last-minute cancel because grief may overwhelm them. Be patient and kind and let them lead.

Honor Their Loved One by Remembering Their Birthday or Anniversary

I cannot tell you how much it blessed me when someone remembered and sent me a text, called, or Facebook message on the birthday of my late husband, my mom, and my dad.

Just yesterday, I received a message from one of my dad's friends saying how much they missed my daddy. Someone remembered a special day in his life. One I had celebrated for over fifty years.

My late husband has been gone for ten years now, and I still have people that were in our wedding, contact me on our anniversary and say sweet things that are healing to my heart. Our lives together mattered.

There are a number of widows and widowers that I reach out to and minister to. I frequently put the anniversary of the day they lost a loved one, their wedding anniversary, or birthday in my phone calendar with an annual reminder. On that day, I try to call, let them know I am thinking about them, and tell them what I loved about the loved one they lost. More than anything, I take time to listen to them, ask them to tell me a story of a special time, or just let them cry because these days trigger grief. I do not have to have the answers; I just need to be with them in their pain and help them through or celebrate with them. It all depends on what they need, and I want to be that friend.

Ask the Grieving Person What They Need When you Spend Time with Them

One of the things I frequently do when spending time either on the phone or in person with someone that has had a loss is tell them I want to be whatever they need in our time together. Sometimes, their conversation quickly dictates what they need, and I feed off of them.

There are other times when I would start our conversation and say, "I want you to let me know what you need today. If you don't want to talk about your struggles and just want to laugh, I can tell you stories and make you laugh. If you need someone to cry with you, I can do that too. And if you just want to talk about normal things, I can also do that."

This gives the grieving person the power and freedom to express what they need at that time, and usually they say something that can let you know how to proceed.

With close friends, I felt free to tell them what I needed when we got together for a walk, a glass of wine, or dinner. None of my close friends had experienced a great loss of parents or mate and asked me to help them understand and tell them what I needed. They wanted to learn.

Grieving people need different things at different times. Sometimes, they really need to share about what they miss, what is hard, and their struggles. They need someone to sit with them in their pain. There were many times I needed to verbalize my pain.

There were other times I just wanted to be normal because there were so many things that were not normal anymore. I longed for something normal, as my normal was gone.

And there were plenty of times I just needed to laugh and have fun because life was so hard. Laughter is good medicine.

You will give your friend a great gift if you ask them what they need when you are with them. It shows sensitivity to where their heart is.

If you are a grieving person, do not be afraid to let those close to you know what you need. If they are truly people that love you, they will want to know so they can help you.

Do not say, "I know exactly how you feel."

I will never forget the day a sweet lady in her eighties made a statement to me. She came into my office and said, "Honey, I'm sorry you lost Joe, and I know exactly how you feel. You will never get over it. I haven't."

Everything in me wanted to scream, "I am forty-nine, and I have a lot of life ahead of me. You don't know how I feel." The truth was she had *some* understanding of where my heart was, but she was much closer to the end of her life than I was.

I am very careful to say to anyone I run into that is grieving, "I have some understanding." This statement honors their unique situation and is closer to the truth. Every situation is different, and there are many factors that contribute to their loss. Some people die after an extended illness, others suddenly or by suicide. Although I have lost a husband, I do not know exactly how someone feels.

**Do not say, "You will have another baby,"
or "You will find another husband."**

After losing the baby I lost, a woman in our community said to me, "It's okay, you have three beautiful children, and you can have another baby." I understand she was trying to help me see the positive side of things, however, those words stung.

I missed the baby I had lost. I wanted *that* baby. My three children did not take away the pain of what I had lost.

I experienced the same comment after losing my late husband. A well-meaning person said, "Kathleen, you are young and beautiful. You will find another man. You'll be a catch for anybody."

Although his words were meant to make me feel better, at that moment, I did not want another husband. I missed the one I had lost.

I learned in all these situations, to simply smile, look at the intent of the words and toss them over my shoulder. They simply were not helpful.

For friends and family of someone who has lost a mate, parent, or child.

Be a Good Listener
Offer Specific Help
Invite the Person for Dinner
Give them Choices—Let them Make Decisions
Honor their Loved One by Remembering their Birthday or Anniversary
Ask the Grieving Person What They Need When you Spend Time with Them
Do Not Say, "I know exactly how you feel"
Do Not Say, "You will have another baby or find another husband"

Chapter 10

Keys to Thriving through
Seasons of Grief

The word thrive is defined as to grow or develop well or vigorously, to flourish. My constant prayer was to not waste the extreme pain my heart went through during waves of grief. Below are some keys I discovered throughout the years of different griefs, that help me grow and thrive.

Keep letting go daily and weekly. I would daily ask God to show me what I needed to let go of today, this week, and this month. Usually something would surface, and I knew it was the thing I needed to release that day or week. This keeps the process moving. There were those days and sometimes weeks where I felt like I got a pass, and it was just a time to rest from the grieving, but for the most part, there was always something to let go of.

Let the tears roll—don't hold them in. Stuffing your emotions will not get you anywhere and will actually backfire on you later on. Crying can be humbling for those of us that like to be strong; however, I found that the unwelcome tears were cleansing for my soul, softened my heart, and gave me greater compassion for others.

Ask God to reveal truth to you. People that are grieving can be deceived by their feelings because their heart is in such turmoil. I would frequently ask God to reveal truth to me in any area my feelings or others had lied to me. I felt like my life was over; however, cognitively, I knew it was not. I was young, knew who I was, had grandchildren to look forward to, and a lot of life to live. Asking God to show me truth helped me to not live in my feelings. My feelings would easily get hurt during waves of grief, and I needed God's truth, especially since I didn't have a husband to bounce things off of. I would also ask God to reveal truth to me because well-meaning people that had never been through grief, said some wrong and hurtful things. I wanted to see clearly and forgive quickly. God's truth is an asset in times of grief.

Keep a notebook of key of information, people that call, etc. because you are forgetful in this season. One of the best things I ever did was buy a fifty-cent spiral notebook. I wrote everything in it from people that called, people I talked to with financial matters, and even my "to do" list. I was extremely forgetful, and the notebook helped me to feel more in control of my life.

Understand that other people will move on in life, but your heart can still be hurting. In the early weeks and months after my loss, many people were close by checking on me, offering help, and were more aware and sensitive of my recent loss. As time progressed, people continued with their lives; however, my heart was still dealing with many things. After losing my husband and right after I passed the one year mark of losing him, a widow mentioned to me that the second year would be harder for me because I would still be working through a lot, and others would forget and go on with their life. I did not want to hear those words; however, she was right, and I am glad she told me because they were helpful. Had she not said those unwanted words, I would have thought I had regressed that second year after my husband's death.

Be patient with yourself, embrace where you are, and realize this is only a season. It is easy to want to rush the grief process because most people do not like the pain their heart is experiencing. I was so eager to move to the next season, especially after losing my husband. I wanted to feel different and be in another place, instead of where I found myself. I was frustrated with myself because I was not moving through the process quicker. I had to learn to be patient with myself. I remember one day, seeing a caregiver assist her client and admired the patience in her. In that moment, I felt God tell me to treat myself with patience. I felt Him say, "You need to be patient with yourself, and you cannot expect yourself to move faster than you are capable of moving in this season. Be kind to yourself, Kathleen, just like that caregiver."

I have encountered numerous widows and widowers that are anxious to move quickly to dating and finding someone else because they are so lonely. I understand that loneliness and was eager to move on; however, the grief was still there and still needed to be worked through. I met a gentleman from another state shortly after my late husband died. He was kind, a good listener, and a friend. Much of our relationship was over the phone, and he helped fill the loneliness at night; however, looking back, I was not really healed and did not have much to give to the relationship. I finally realized that and some months down the road, we ended our dating relationship. I had to learn to be patient with myself and give my heart time to heal, keeping my eyes on the fact that this was only a season in my life, and it would pass.

When we try to be strong and pretend we do not hurt, we only hinder and prolong the process. Grief will have its way. Embracing it and partnering with it is best.

A balanced life is a big key. There is so much to do when you have lost your mate or partner. Your life is suddenly adjusted and things that were once shared, are now your sole responsibility. I found I could not focus too much on one thing as it was not beneficial. I needed to spend time dealing with the grief, supporting myself, and paying bills. I also needed to get death certificates to necessary places, go through my husband's things, deal with investments, and simply have fun again. If I worked on any one of these things too much, I lost my balance and peace in my life. It was not good for me to pour all my energy into work, spend all my time working through the grief, focus only on house cleaning, etc., or play all the time. I needed to do a little of all of those things.

> Balance is key when you are going through intense seasons of grief. It helps you navigate better.

Focus on one day at a time. Sometimes, looking back at all we lost is too much to dwell on, and looking at the rest of our life without the person we have lost is overwhelming. I found I did much better simply looking at the day in front of me, one day at a time. How was I going to get through that day? There was grace for that day and whatever I needed to deal with. I remember one day, I was in tears trying to figure out how I could possibly go forward without my late husband. I muttered the words, "Lord, I don't have enough strength." In that moment, I felt God say, "I don't give you a package of strength, I give you strength as you walk with me each day." Those words settled my heart that was tempted to be overwhelmed.

> Asking God to adjust your lens and give you His perspective will be helpful.

It is very easy to only see your own pain and what you have lost. It is easy to feel like your life is over, and you will never get over your grief and quit crying. It seems to come naturally to focus on the negative in your life. I know for me, I struggled with all of the above. This was not leading me in a positive direction, so one day, I came across a scripture that helped me readjust my focus. Isaiah 55: 8–9 (NIV) states, "For my thoughts are not your thoughts, neither are your ways my ways," declares the Lord. "As the heavens are higher than the earth, so are my ways higher than your ways and my thoughts than your thoughts."

I asked God to show me His perspective of my life and how He saw it. I felt God say, "You have lots of adventure ahead of you." This gave me hope and something to look forward to. Somehow, reframing my life through this lens of adventure, helped keep me expectant about my future. I can now tell you, ten years later, I have had lots of adventure. I have done many new things I never did before. I highly recommend trying new things when you find your life in ashes. Trying new things helped me to build new memories, depend on God in a fresh and fun way, and showed me I was much more capable than I imagined. Seeing each day or new event that might seem daunting as an adventure with God helped me build a new life.

Be willing to try new things and be open to learning new skills. I had to step out of my comfort zone. One of the new things I tried was swing dancing lessons. A couple from my church invited me to go with them to San Antonio, Texas, each Monday evening for lessons. In this setting, you do not have to have a partner. You rotate in a circle and dance with different people. I learned a lot about dealing with men in a safe setting, and the exercise was great. I also got brave and began dating. Dating at fifty looked very different than it was thirty-three years ago. In each situation, when I simply looked to God to be my protector of my heart and body and saw each date as an adventure with God, as well as an opportunity to get to know someone new; it made things easier. A little over two years after my late husband was gone, I began dating my current husband, Stephen. He was different than my previous husband in some ways and similar in other ways. I began to love the differences as I was not looking for someone like my late husband. He was gone, and I knew I would exhaust myself trying to find someone just like him. I learned to fish and hunt with Stephen and discovered I love it!

Kathleen dove hunting with her husband, Stephen

Kathleen's new life fishing

Kathleen and Stephen—new life

Hang on to hope in the dark days and remember that this is only a season. When grief rolls over you, and the deep pain of it brings things to the surface, it is easy to feel like we will never be happy again. We will feel the ache in our heart, and we can find ourselves gasping for breath. In these times, we need to hang on to hope. Hebrews 6:18 (NIV) tells us, "We who have fled to take hold of the hope offered us may be greatly encouraged. We have this hope as an anchor for the soul, firm and secure." Hope helps keep us steady and not tossed around by our emotions. I would frequently say to myself out loud, "God, my hope is in you and this is only a season." I needed to hear those words.

Adventure is your secret weapon. Adventure is engaging in an exciting activity, especially the exploration of unknown territory. When you have been in a relationship or marriage for a long time and your significant other or mate is no longer with you, life can be daunting. Simply going to events alone, instead of always having a date, can be challenging. Dating, traveling alone, or buying a car by yourself are suddenly major events and can be a little scary. One day, I asked God how He saw the things I was having to do alone and how I could look at them and not be overwhelmed. I knew fear was not from God, so how did He see them? I felt Him say, "See everything as an adventure with me. I will be with you." As I navigated through these new things alone, I began to get excited as I was on an adventure with God. It took the fear out of the unknown. When I first began to date, I remember praying and saying, "God, protect my heart, body, and mind, and show me if this guy is for me." God was faithful. I dated several men before remarrying, and it was always comforting to know God was with me.

I made myself step out of my comfort zone and do things that were new. I planned a trip to Cabo San Lucas, Mexico, with a girl-friend, and that was a big adventure. I saw new places, tried different foods, and simply learned to laugh again. When the fear of doing something alone would hit me, I immediately began to reframe that thought with seeing it through the lens of adventure. It took the sting out of the unknown.

I needed a new car and had never bought my own car. I began to see this new task as an adventure and began to pray about what to buy, cost, etc. I asked a friend that was a car dealer to find me a convertible Toyota Solara. One day, he called and said he had found the perfect car, and that I could come test-drive it. It looked exactly like what I wanted. As I pulled away from the dealership, I prayed, asking God to clearly show me if this car was for me. I drove to my house, checked my mail, and saw an envelope from the company my late husband worked for. In the mail, was a bonus check from the company, and it was exactly the amount of money I needed for the new car! It was pretty clear; this was the vehicle I was to have, and God revealed that He was with me in my adventure.

I have had countless adventures with God since I first began to see things through the lens of adventure. I would sometimes feel like Indiana Jones in some of his adventure movies. This perspective was much more motivating to deal with life's uncertainties than coddling fear and staying stuck in decision making. To this day, I still use "my adventure lens" when anything daunting comes along. I am forever thankful for all I have learned in my seasons of grief.

Step out, make plans with people and initiate connection. The heart takes time to heal. Remember, people will go on with their life and can forget where your heart is. Let me encourage you to be an initiator. This may take you out of your comfort zone, but it is worth it. Remember, you are responsible for your healing, not others. Do not sit around in self-pity and wait for others to ask you out, over to dinner or to an event. Do not wait for your kids to invite you over, call and invite them to your house. They have busy lives and often can be dealing with their own problems or grief, or are raising a family. All of us love to be invited to something, but what if God is wanting you to initiate things, reach out and make new friends and memories? Again, you are responsible for your own healing, not others.

You have a God-given right to be healed. One of the things I realized in my grief was that God understood my pain. He sent Jesus to heal me and the Holy Spirit to comfort, teach, and lead me out of grief. John 14:26–27 (NIV) says, "But the Counselor, the Holy Spirit, whom the Father will send in my name, will teach you all things and remind you of everything I have said to you." Jesus paid a great price by dying on the cross to carry my sorrow. My heart did not heal overnight; it was a process, just like healing from a surgery. Ten years down the road, it was easy to see, God was right there with me every step of the way, healing me day by day.

> Pray for grief to have a good work in you and ask God to keep you moving in the process.

One of my constant prayers was for grief to have a good work in my life. Although I did not necessarily like the process, I did not want to waste it. I wanted the pain and anguish my heart was going through to work negative things out of my life and good, positive things into my life. Somehow, I felt like I was giving birth to some-thing new. Giving birth to my three children was not easy; it was painful, but they were all worth it. My daily prayer was, "God, I want grief to have a good work in me and keep me moving through the process. Please do not let me get stuck."

Choose to live with the questions. There are going to be things we just don't understand until we get to heaven. I think that is why God says over and over in the Bible to trust Him. I love a quote by author Graham Cooke, which says, "God often allows in his wisdom, what he could prevent in his power." When my mother got very sick and began to decline, it was very difficult for me. I really struggled with the "why" question. Why did she get sick now? Why didn't God heal her? I had just stepped into full time ministry and my sweet mama, who had prayed for me all my life, was not there for me when I needed her the most. I went to a friend and began to talk about the situation. The advice he gave was, "Kathleen, the question is can you trust God if you never get an answer?" I had to ponder the question for a while, and finally concluded, I could choose to trust God even if I never received an answer to my question. I made an active choice to live with the question. I strongly suggest you make a choice to live with the question. I discovered the why question can keep you stuck. When my late husband was diagnosed with cancer, I never asked why. I had learned from the experience with my mom, and I did not have time to waste. Perhaps one day I will understand why God took Joe at such an early age, but until then, my heart is at rest, and I can trust God.

Get help when you need it. Perhaps one of the most difficult things to do is to ask others for help. Grief puts us in a state of simply needing help at times to move forward in life. Sometimes we need physical assistance, and other times it is emotional or spiritual help that we need. The obstacle that stands in our way is pride. Do not let your pride be a stumbling block in your life. All of us need help at one time or another. When you are in a season of grief, ask trusted people in your life for help. Most will be happy to assist you if you tell them specifically what you need or how you are struggling. If they cannot help, perhaps they can direct you to someone that can. When I was deep in the early stages of grief after losing my husband, I had little or no appetite due to the emotions I was wrestling with. Dinner was difficult because I was not used to eating alone. One evening, I called my friend Tammy and asked her to please come over. I confessed that I had not eaten much in the recent days and knew I needed to eat. I needed accountability to keep moving forward. She was at my house in thirty minutes and visited with me and I ate. Yes, this was humbling, as I am usually a strong woman that loves to eat. I just needed help to move forward physically and emotionally. Since that time, I have had many widows contact me when they encounter a tough wave of grief. I am happy to spend time with them, to help them move forward in their lives.

Hang on to hope. There are many days when you are walking through grief that life can seem overwhelming and you feel like you will never be yourself again. In these days, hang on to hope. Hope anchors our soul. Hebrews 6:19 (NIV) states, "We have this hope as an anchor of our soul, firm and secure." Sometimes I would write different reminders and put them in key places in my home, office, or car to remind me to hang on to God and hope. Another scripture that was key for me was Jeremiah 29:11 (NIV), which says, "For I know the plans I have for you," declares the Lord, "plans to prosper you and not to harm you, plans to give you hope and a future."

Psalms 130 is another scripture that gave me great hope as I waited for a new season to come. Grief takes time and energy and you cannot rush it. When we wait on God and put our hope in Him, our time is not wasted.

Psalms 130:7 (NIV) states, "O Israel, put your hope in the Lord, for with the Lord is unfailing love and with him is full redemption."

I have seen God's redemption over and over in my life, especially in times of grief. Sometimes it has taken a while, but He has redeemed each situation in time. As I have continued to look to God and wait on Him, much has been worked into my life and much has been worked out. All of these changes have made me a better person.

Keys to Thriving Through Seasons of Grief

- *Keep letting go daily and weekly.*

- *Let the tears roll—don't hold them in.*

- *Ask God to reveal truth to you. People that are grieving can be deceived by their feelings because their heart is in such turmoil.*

- *Keep a notebook of key of information, people that call, etc. because you are forgetful in this season.*

- *Understand that other people will move on in life, but your heart can still be hurting.*

- *Be patient with yourself, embrace where you are, and realize this is only a season.*

- *A balanced life is a big key.*

- *Focus on one day at a time.*

- *Be willing to try new things and be open to learning new skills.*

- *Hang on to hope in the dark days and remember that this is only a season.*

- *Adventure is your secret weapon.*

- *Step out, make plans with people and initiate connection.*

- *You have a God-given right to be healed.*

- *Choose to live with the questions.*

- *Get help when you need it.*

- *Hang on to hope.*

Chapter 11

God's Promises for us in our Grief

(Let me encourage you to pick several of these promises each month and write them on an index card. Put the cards in places where you will frequently see them to remind you of God's promises for you. I suggest putting them in places like in your car, on your refrigerator, at your desk, in your bathroom, etc.)

Widows and those that have lost their father are near and dear to the heart of God.

"A father to the fatherless, a defender of widows, is God in his holy dwelling. God sets the lonely in families, he leads out the prisoners with singing…" *(Psalms 68:5–6, NIV).*

You are promised joy in the days ahead. Keep pressing on in your tears.

"Those who sow in tears shall reap with songs of joy" *(Psalm 126:5, NIV).*

God will bind up your broken heart. Keep taking it to Him.

"The Spirit of the Sovereign Lord is on me because the Lord has anointed me to proclaim good news to the poor. He has sent me to bind up the brokenhearted, to proclaim freedom for the captives and release from darkness for the prisoners, to proclaim the year of the Lord's favor and the day of vengeance of our God, to comfort all who mourn, and provide for those who grieve in Zion to bestow on them a crown of beauty instead of ashes, the oil of joy instead of mourning and a garment of praise instead of a spirit of despair. They will be called oaks of righteousness, a planting of the Lord for the display of his splendor." *(Isaiah 61:1–3 NIV)*

God will protect you and send those to be your advocate.

"Learn to do right! Seek justice, encourage the oppressed. Defend the cause of the fatherless, plead the case of the widow" *(Isaiah 1:17, NIV)*.

God will comfort you. Run to Him. Then, He will use you to comfort others.

"Praise be to God and Father of our Lord Jesus Christ, the Father of compassion and the God of all comfort, who comforts us in all our trouble, so that we can comfort those in any trouble, with the comfort we ourselves have received from God." *(2 Corinthians 1:4, NIV)*

THRIVING THROUGH SEASONS OF GRIEF

You will pass through your grief and tears. It is not your destination, and it will become a place of strength for you.

"Blessed are those whose strength is in you, whose hearts are set on pilgrimage. As they pass through the Valley of Baka, they make it a place of springs; the autumn rains also cover it with pools. They go from strength to strength, till each appears before God in Zion." (*Psalms 84:5–7*, NIV)

God's grace is all you need. His power will help you through this time.

But he said to me, "My grace is sufficient for you, for my power is made perfect in weakness. Therefore I will boast all the more gladly about my weaknesses, so that Christ's power may rest on me."(*2 Corinthians 12:9* NIV)

God's power will sustain you. Sustain means to strengthen, uphold and affirm.

"The Lord watches over the foreigner and sustains the fatherless and the widow but he frustrates the ways of the wicked" (*Psalms 146:9*, NIV).

God will heal your broken heart.

"He heals the brokenhearted and binds up their wounds" (*Psalms 147:3*, NIV).

God will comfort you, make your life a beautiful garden, and give you joy.

The Lord will surely comfort Zion and look with compassion on all her ruins; he will make her deserts like Eden, her wastelands like the garden of the Lord. Joy and gladness will be found in her, thanksgiving and the sound of singing. (*Isaiah 51:2–3*, NIV)

God has good plans for you.
"For I know the plans I have for you," declares the Lord, "plans to prosper you and not to harm you, plans to give you hope and a future" (*Jeremiah 29:11*, NIV).

You are dearly loved, and God will build from the ruins of your life. You will find joy again.

"I have loved you with an everlasting love; I have drawn you with lovingkindness. I will build you up again and you will be rebuilt... Again you will take up your tambourines and go out to dance with the joyful" (Jeremiah 31:3–4, NIV).

God will turn your mourning into dancing.

"They will be like a well-watered garden, and they will sorrow no more. Then maddens will dance and be glad, young men and old as well. I will turn their mourning into gladness; I will give them comfort and joy instead of sorrow." (*Jeremiah 31:12–13*, NIV)

There is hope for your future.

"This is what the Lord says: restrain your voice from weeping and your eyes from tears, for your work will be rewarded," declares the Lord...

"So there is hope for your future," declares the Lord (*Jeremiah 31:16–17*).

You are guaranteed joy.

"So with you: Now is your time of grief, but I will see you again and you will rejoice, and no one will take away your joy" (John 16:22, NIV).

You are precious to God. God will deal with those that are unkind to you.

"Do not take advantage of a widow or an orphan. If you do and they cry out to me, I will certainly hear their cry" (Exodus 22:22, NIV).

God will light your path, guide you and your sorrow will end.

"...the Lord will be your everlasting light; and your days of sorrow will end" (*Isaiah 60:20*, NIV).

God will help you.

"Give proper recognition to those widows who are really in need. But if a widow has children or grandchildren, these should learn first of all to put their religion into practice by caring for their own family and so repaying their parents and grandparents, for this is pleasing to God. The widow who is really in need and left all alone puts her hope in God and continues night and day to pray and to ask God for help." (*1 Timothy 5:3–5*, NIV)

God will hold your hand.

"For I am the Lord your God who takes hold of your right hand and says to you, Do not fear; I will help you" (*Isaiah 41:13,* NIV).

God will sustain you when you cry out to Him.

"Surely God is my help; the Lord is the one who sustains me" (*Psalms 54:4,* NIV).

God will walk you through your dark valley and comfort you.

"Yea, though I walk through the valley of the shadow of death, I will fear no evil: for thou art with me; thy rod and thy staff they comfort me" (*Psalms 23:4,* KJV).

God understands your suffering and will be with you when you are misunderstood.

"He was despised and rejected by mankind, a man of suffering, and familiar with pain. Like one from whom people hide their faces he was despised, and we held him in low esteem. Surely, he took up our pain and bore our suffering, yet we considered him punished by God, stricken by him, and afflicted. But he was pierced for our transgressions, he was crushed for our iniquities; the punishment that brought us peace was on him, and by his wounds we are healed." (*Isaiah 53:3–5,* NIV)

God understands our groaning and tears.

"I am worn out from my groaning. All night long I flood my bed with weeping and drench my couch with tears. My eyes grow weak with sorrow they; fail because of all my foes" (*Psalms 6:6–7*, NIV).

God seeks after you and you belong.

"I will not leave you as orphans; I will come to you" (*John 14:18*, NIV).

God will counsel you, teach you and help you.

"But the Counselor, the Holy Spirit, whom the Father will send in my name, will teach you all things and remind you of everything I have said to you" (*John 14:26–27*, NIV).

God will be your father.

"I will be a Father to you, and you will be my sons and daughters, says the Lord Almighty" (2 Corinthians 6:18, NIV).

When our father and mother are gone, God takes over.

"Though my father and mother forsake me, the Lord will receive me" (Psalms 27:10, NIV).

You belong to God.

"How great is the love the Father has lavished on us, that we should be called children of God! And that is what we are!" (*1 John 3:1*, NIV)

God will deliver you from your distress and lead you.

"Then they cried out to the Lord in their trouble, and he delivered them from their distress. He led them by a straight way to a city where they could settle" (Psalms 107:6–7, NIV).

God places great value on widows and orphans.

"Religion that God our Father accepts as pure and faultless is this: to look after orphans and widows in their distress and to keep oneself from being polluted by the world" (James 1:27, NIV).

Kathleen and son Austin

Christmas 2019

Kathleen and Stephen's blended family in 2018

Chapter 12

Crafted Prayer for Times and Seasons of Grief

A crafted prayer is a prayer where you sit and ask God what is in His heart for you for a particular situation. Below is a crafted prayer I wrote in one of my seasons of grief. Feel free to use it for your own life or ask God to give you one for your situation. A crafted prayer is a way to partner with God and move through the grief process.

Crafted Prayer for Times and Seasons of Grief

Lord, I look to you and thank you for being with me in this season of grief

I declare grief will have a good work in my life and will not be wasted

I choose to partner with you to work things into me and work things out of me

You, and only you, are my healer, I look to you and give you my pain

Help me to see things from your perspective and my life as an adventure with you

Thank you for who I am as I walk with you and depend on you. Amen

White Flag of Surrender Wave
By Elyssa Faith Danielson

It is okay to grieve for the loss of change,
It is significant, poignant, sharp.
It is a glaringly white flag of surrender
That you wave bravely in the wind,
And as you look up at it, you weep.
You weep partly from relief:
This battle, at least, is near over.
You weep partly from exhaustion:
This battle has been long and rough.
You weep partly because you are different now:
You have changed in the struggle,
And in the aftermath of the battle,
All life has a new hue, a new smell, a new texture.
Hold there, in that recognition of newness,
Hold.
Weep.
Fall
And be caught by the merciful Combat Medic.
Breathe.
Breathe.
Breathe.
Be held.
Weep.

He understands the loss in its entirety.
He has felt the weight and wept too.
Hold and be held until He tells you to move.
It may be briefer or longer than you expect,
But He knows the proper time and ways.
Breathe. Weep. Hold. Be held. Stand
Stronger now, softer now, wiser now,
For having endured, even if you were shaking.
He will walk with you into the new day,
Into the time of rest and rejoicing,
Into the end of things and the grand, foretold,
Miraculous new beginning.

Instagram: @elyssafaith

Resources

Keys to Letting Go and Ways to Say Goodbye

- *Cry and pour your heart out to God. Let the tears roll when you are alone and when you are in public. Tears are a natural release of your grief. They are healing, and you never have to apologize for them.*

- *Write a letter to yourself, God or a person or season of life. Journaling is a great way to process your feelings.*

- *Choose to forgive. You may need to forgive the person for dying and leaving you, forgive a spouse for leaving the marriage, forgive God, or forgive the person that took their life. Forgiveness keeps our heart soft. Pray, "God, I choose as an act of my will to forgive. Change my heart and heal it."*

- *Admit when your heart hurts. My prayer looked something like this, "Lord, this still hurts. I open my heart to you. Please heal me." This is not denying or medicating our pain. It is embracing it.*

Important Things to Remember About Grief

- *It is a process and cannot be rushed.*

- *Honor the pain, but don't live in it.*

- *The greater the love/relationship and investment in your life, the longer the process takes.*

- *The important thing with grief is to keep moving through it.*

- *If grief is not dealt with initially, it will resurface.*

- *Our feelings can lie to us in times of grief.*

- *The beauty of grief is that it can work things into us and out of us.*

- *Grief will come like waves in the ocean. Do not be disillusioned that you are not making progress when one hits.*

- *Grief is a time of transition. The purpose of transition is to move us from one place to another.*

- *No grief experience is exactly the same.*

- *You, not others, are responsible for your healing.*

- *Grief can exaggerate fear.*

- *Anniversaries, special days, places, and holidays can often trigger grief.*

Keys to Thriving Through Seasons of Grief

- *Keep letting go daily and weekly.*

- *Let the tears roll—don't hold them in.*

- *Ask God to reveal truth to you. People that are grieving can be deceived by their feeling because their heart is in such turmoil.*

- *Keep a notebook of key of information, people that call, etc. because you are forgetful in this season.*

- *Understand that other people will move on in life, but your heart can still be hurting.*

- *Be patient with yourself, embrace where you are, and realize that this is only a season.*

- *A balanced life is a big key.*

- *Focus on one day at a time.*

- *Be willing to try new things and be open to learning new skills.*

- *Hang on to hope in the dark days and remember, "this is only a season."*

- *Adventure is your secret weapon.*

- *Step out, make plans with people and initiate connection.*

- *You have a God given right to be healed.*

- *Choose to live with the questions.*

- *Get help when you need it.*

- *Hang on to hope.*

For friends and family of someone who has lost a mate, parent, or child

- *Be a good listener*

- *Offer specific help*

- *Invite the person for dinner*

- *Give them choices—let them make decisions*

- *Honor their loved one by remembering their birthday or anniversary*

- *Ask the grieving person what they need when you spend time with them*

- *Do not say, "I know exactly how you feel." Do not say, "You will have another baby," or "You will find another husband."*

Crafted Prayer for Times and Seasons of Grief

Lord, I look to you and thank you for being with me in this season of grief.

I declare grief will have a good work in my life and will not be wasted.

I choose to partner with you to work things into me and work things out of me.

You, and only you, are my healer, I look to you and give you my pain.

Help me to see things from your perspective and my life as an adventure with you.

Thank you for who I am as I walk with you and depend on you. Amen.

(This prayer can be cut out and placed where frequently seen.)

About the Author

Kathleen Maxwell-Rambie

A Kerrville, Texas native, Kathleen joins her passion for the Lord and compassion for those in need.

Her career as a business owner and educator eventually led to her calling as an executive director of a nonprofit, helping women in need and later, helping young adults establish positive lifestyles. She also served as a development officer of a global nonprofit.

She is a regular columnist for several Texas newspapers and is also a blogger and podcaster, reaching around the world with her blog, www.themaxwellminutes.blogspot.com and podcast, www.kathleenmaxwellrambie.podbean.com.

Kathleen enjoys speaking and is passionate about helping people discover their value and worth. She shares transparently from her life's challenges, bringing hope, joy and lessons on how to walk each day with God in our lives.

She leads a community Bible study in Kerrville, Texas, bringing people from various churches together called The Gathering-Bringing God into Everyday Life. She has spoken internationally, as well as at conferences, churches, and community events. She speaks on the topic of grief and how it has been her best teacher. She also shares about the losses in her life and about finding new life again.

She and her husband, Stephen, have five adult children and eight adorable grandchildren together. Since their marriage in 2012, they enjoy spending time with family, traveling, dancing, hunting, fishing, entertaining, and the outdoors.

www.kathleenmaxwellrambie.com
www.themaxwellminutes.blogspot.com
kathleenmaxwellrambie.podbean.com podcast (Understanding and Releasing Heartbreak, Dealing with Life's Disappointments, Freedom from Fear, Seeing God in the Transitions of Life, Walking in Peace, Trusting God with What Matters in Life)
kathleenmaxwell1@gmail.com